MW01200424

INVISIBLE HISTORY

INVISIBLE HISTORY

THE COLLECTED POEMS OF WALTA BORAWSKI

edited by
Philip Clark *&* Michael Bronski

THE LIBRARY OF HOMOSEXUAL CONGRESS
NEW ORLEANS

Published in the United States of America by
Library of Homosexual Congress
An imprint of Rebel Satori Press
www.rebelsatoripress.com

Cover photograph: Walta Borawski, September 1987, by Robert Giard. Robert Giard Papers. Yale Collection of American Literature, Beinecke Rare Book and Manuscript Library. Copyright The Estate of Robert Giard; used by courtesy of Jonathan Silin.

Photo inside back cover: Michael Bronski and Walta Borawski, September 1987, by Robert Giard. Robert Giard Papers. Yale Collection of American Literature, Beinecke Rare Book and Manuscript Library. Copyright The Estate of Robert Giard; used by courtesy of Jonathan Silin.

Hardcover ISBN: 978-1-60864-241-0
Paperback ISBN: 978-1-60864-239-7

Library of Congress Control Number: 2022948503

Contents

Acknowledgments   i

Introduction   iii

Sexually Dangerous Poet (1984)

Cheers, Cheers for Old Cha Cha Ass   1

Trying to Write a Love Poem   3

Wool-gathering   5

For Michael, on the brink of depression & war.   8

The Autobiographies of Utensils   9

(No title)   10

Christmas on Long Island, 1977   11

On Seeing One's Self, Years Later, in an Inexpensive Restaurant   15

Role Model   17

My Mother Was a Seamstress   19

From a Winter's Notebook   20

St. Theresa of Hemenway Street   25

After Doing Coke at Steve's Goodbye Party   28

Valentine's Day 1981   30

Three Poems from the Pompeii Exhibit   31

Aborted Adonis   35

Normal as Two Ships in the Night   37

bez tyutu*   39

Gentility   40

Traveling in the Wrong Century   41

Power of One   42

Live Free or Die   44

Travel Fatigue #2   45

Tired Song-&-Dance Act   47
My Perfect Poetry Reading   48
Some of Us Are Stretched Tighter Than Others   50
God, the unplucked notes.   52
Direct or Indirect Rebound Tenderness   56
Surprising Kisses   57
Hunger   59
Sociologically Challenged   61
For Emily Dickinson & Charley Shively: 63
Perversity   64
Salome   65
Against Sex   66
It's Earth Wars Worry Me   68
If I Ran Harvard University…   71
I am not Billie Holiday...   72
Indexing Judy Garland's Life...   74
Sullivan   76
Things Are Still Sudden & Wonderful   78

Uncollected Poems

[stick it in sweet man mine]   81
A Harmless Tail   82
[For those who arrived too early or too late]   84
Thanksgiving Weekend, 1976   85
Dead Languages   88
[Relationships have boundaries]   89
[All in white but loveless & without music]   90
[Harvard has no class these days; nothing does]   91
Didn't That Bother You   92
Voyeur   95

Instant   97
Loveability Zero   99
On the Roof   101
Cruising Athletes from a Sunny Window in Lamont   102
Shame   105
The Marks of Fairy Tales   106
The Poet Falls, Flags & Willowtrees   107
Silk Scarves & Hard Leather   109
Circles Might Lead to Rectangular Beds, Straight Lines Don't   110
Some of Us Wear Pink Triangles   111
Invisible History   113
Neurotic Singlet   115
Still Life, with Dull Glow   116
Finding Appropriate Gestures   117
Whimsical Spring Poem (Harvard Man I)   118

Lingering in a Silk Shirt (1994)
Ragged Denim

Jude   123
Propriety   124
1969   125
Fragrances and Carcinogens   127
Sleep and Trust   128
Art and Remembrance   129
For Carl Wittman   130
Cornwall's Servant   131
There are no snapshots of my mother...   132
Eminent Domain   133
Rationale   136
Choice   138

Serious Irises   139
Arnold   140
In Style Again   141
The Luck of the Draw   142
Calendar   143
Driving the Stake Through My Father's Heart   145
Visitation & Mortality   146
Twins   147

Nylon Lycra

New Brunswick   153
Frank O'Hara Homage at Harvard   154
Artistry & Hypochondria   156
For Mitzel   157
For Tipper Gore   159
Legend Has It   161
Watching Sting on *Saturday Night Live*   162
While Looking at a Photograph of Barbra Streisand...   163
Vision of Love   165
Sooner or Later   166
For John Wieners   167
New Paltz 1991   168

The J. Poems

Things I Cannot Bring You   171
I Know Your Name   172
Tribute   175
Dishes   176
7 Embarrassments in the Wrong Key   177
Outlaws of Love   181

Simple Gifts   182
On Your Guard   183
Therapy   185
Wardrobe   186
Incorrigible   187
8:30 a.m.   188
Last Year   189
Muscle Psyche   191
In the Order   192
Sanctus   193
Worship   194
Figurant   195
After Reading an Alfred Chester Story   196
Never Ever   197
Occluded Front   199
Riverside Cambridgeport, Winter   201
Reality Check   202
Fin   204

Blue Rayon
Diagnosis   207
Breakfast in the 1990s   208
The Mouth Poem   210
Away   211
Transition in *Newsweek*   213
Empowerment   215
When Jim Died   216
Talking to Jim   218
The Robert Mapplethorpe Quartet   219
Twilight   223

Brothers   224
Celebrating the State of Non-virus   225
Garden Mystery   227
Chance   228
I dreamed   229
virus cutting   230
The Gentleman and the Lady in Me   231

Coda:
Walta Borawski's Final Poem
Writing with AIDS   235
[Michael I miss you so much]   237

Afterword   245
Biographical Note   251

Acknowledgments

Michael Bronski's Acknowledgments

Acknowledgments are a publication formality that feel, at least to me, difficult to articulate in this volume. Having lived with some of these poems for nearly half a century they are part of a life and legacy that I am immensely grateful are back in print. The poems in this book might never have seen the light of day—or even been written—if Walta had not been part of a vibrant community of activists, friends, and artists who created the world that allowed him to write and publish. Of all these people, special thanks goes to Charley Shively who, while always working with ever-changing collectives of dedicated writers and thinkers, was instrumental in keeping both *Fag Rag* and Good Gay Poets going. Walta's poems appeared in the former, and his books were published by the latter. These people and groups made Walta's work possible. Thanks to Jonathan Silin and the Robert Giard Foundation for their generous permission to reprint two of Robert Giard's photos in this book. Special thanks to Patrick Merla who in 2001 featured Walta's poetry in *The James White Review* where it found a new audience. Finally, I need to thank the artistic vision of Philip Clark, whose relentless and unflagging dedication to this work make this book possible as well as to Tom Cardamone who was instrumental in bringing it into print.

Philip Clark's Acknowledgments

From the time I was a teenager, Michael Bronski has supported my interest in Walta Borawski's poetry, sending me copies of both published collections and encouraging my work to bring Walta's words back to public attention. I first proposed the idea of Walta's collected poems in

2005, and he has been extraordinarily patient as the road to publication diverged in many different directions.

When he was writer-in-residence at the College of William & Mary, Chris Bram learned of my enthusiasm for Walta's work and immediately introduced me to Michael. He has ever after been the greatest believer in me and the best possible example of a public-spirited and generous writer and scholar. We never run out of things to talk about, do we, Chris?

Nick Mroczek in Minneapolis and Stephen Wilder and David Cobb Craig in New York City provided accommodations where this collection and its introductory essay were initially planned. Jim Cory talked with me about Walta's poetry and (without necessarily knowing it) provided inspiration for the introductory essay. Many thanks to them all.

Thanks to Sven Davisson, Tom Cardamone, and everyone at Rebel Satori who has contributed to publishing this collection. Special thanks to Tom for soliciting my suggestions for Rebel Satori's new Library of Homosexual Congress imprint. Here's to the recovery of important gay literature before any more becomes invisible history. I look forward to future collaborations.

Introduction

The Histories of Walta Borawski
by Philip Clark

Let us begin at the end, both of the poet's life and this collection of his work. Turn to the very last pages of *Invisible History: The Collected Poems of Walta Borawski*, the pages I suspect few read carefully in most books: the bibliographical notes. Walta's publication history shows that, at the time of his death from AIDS in February 1994, his poems had appeared in a half-dozen anthologies. In the four years following his passing, he appeared in a half-dozen more, including books released by mainstream publishers like St. Martin's and Crown. In the twenty-three years since: near invisibility. David Groff and I included a handful of poems when we edited *Persistent Voices: Poetry by Writers Lost to AIDS* (2009), and Patrick Merla and I published selections of work in, respectively, the *James White Review* in 2001 and the *William & Mary Review* in 2003. Otherwise, Walta's poetic voice, the embodiment of his history, has gone silent.

To what should we attribute this neglect? Part of it seems natural, the usual gaps that widen in the wake of a writer's absence. Walta's poems appeared in small-circulation poetry magazines or long-defunct gay journals and newspapers. His two books, *Sexually Dangerous Poet* and *Lingering in a Silk Shirt*, are out-of-print and the collectives that published them have disbanded. Audiences can forget the vitality of a poet's work when he is no longer present to promote it. But I believe there is more to the story, factors related to Walta's style and to the era in which he lived and that his poems reflect.

To begin, while this poetry works on the page, the full effect of what Allen Ginsberg called Walta's "mindful measure of spoken speech music" is only achieved when heard aloud. It shares this quality with modern-day slam and performance poetry—never the most critically-acclaimed or anthologized genres, and requiring a performer of skill and nuance to achieve success. These are not passive poems. They were not written to win acclaim from poetry professors or to earn the poet an MFA or a teaching gig. The poems glow with intelligence, but they are no mere intellectual exercises; they come, too, from the heart, and the gut, and sometimes from the groin. Walta is no longer here to present them, and they require the energy of being read aloud. If you're unwilling to do so, put this book down. There are other poets.

Walta's work also spans two major periods in gay community life that have been neglected because they are either unpleasant to remember or not simple to assimilate into today's dominant ideals. The poems in *Sexually Dangerous Poet*, along with the uncollected pieces gathered in this volume, fall squarely, not into current gay rights rhetoric, but into the 1970s era of Gay Liberation. They appeared in such gay-specific publications as *Fag Rag*, *Gay Community News*, and *Mouth of the Dragon*. Poems like "Didn't That Bother You," "Instant, "Surprising Kisses," and "Hunger" derive from a period when cruising for sex in streets, porno theaters, baths, and toilets was commonplace in large urban areas like Borawski's Boston (and, although it's rarely discussed, many smaller cities and towns throughout the country). There are poems, such as "Trying to Write a Love Poem," dedicated to

> *the man who stole white lilacs from*
> *Harvard to help me find spring in a*
> *dull season*

—Walta's long-time partner, cultural critic Michael Bronski—but as even Walta admitted,

> *most of my words go to describe*
> *loves that fail, tricks who come & go.*
>
> "Trying to Write a Love Poem"

(It should be noted, however, that Walta had little interest in sex without affection and rejected the politics of exclusion—no fats, no femmes, no S&M, no older men—so prevalent in the gay community then and now. See, for example, the poem-cum-manifesto "Against Sex" for details.) Coming from an era when gay male promiscuity was seen as an act of liberation following years of sexual repression, this refrain in Walta's poetry sits uneasily beside the current public emphasis on gay marriage and monogamy. His involvement in the Boston-based radical collective Fag Rag ensures that neither does his poetry match the other M-word concerns of the gay community in the years since his death: military service and making money.

Meanwhile, Walta's approaching death from AIDS sits as a specter over his second book, *Lingering in a Silk Shirt*. Gay life and gay literature of the mid-1980s to mid-1990s was dominated by discussion of AIDS, but two years following Walta's death, the welcome introduction of protease inhibitors dramatically slowed the disease's toll in the United States. Exhausted from the fight for survival and its accompanying mental strain, few wanted to read any more about AIDS. Walta's later poems fell into a lengthy period of relative silence about the disease in the gay literary world. As conservative forces from both outside and within the community blamed AIDS on gay men's sexual adventurousness during the 1970s and '80s, Walta's liberatory vision found less ground on which to stand.

With enough time and distance, however, there has been a resurgence of interest in the lives and art of those lost to AIDS. Work has recently been reprinted, revived, and written about. This has ranged from writers

(Tim Dlugos, Donald Britton, Steve Abbott, Robert Ferro, Assotto Saint) to visual artists (David Wojnarowicz, Mark Morrisroe, Patrick Angus, Larry Stanton, Marlon Riggs) to activists (witness the surge of documentaries, histories, and oral histories of ACT-UP). Walta deserves similar reclamation. Let us begin at the beginning.

Personal History

Walta Borawski was born in 1947 in the Long Island town of Patchogue to parents who were a butcher and a seamstress. Intellectual, passionate, effeminate, he was an awkward fit in both his family and hometown. A father who thought his boy

> *should try hard to be*
> *more like Rory Calhoun*

was not going to be satisfied with a son who insisted

> *I still intend*
> *to be Elizabeth Taylor*
> "Role Model"

Neither was the "circle of charming boys" at Patchogue High, whose daily torture of him retrospectively spurred one of Walta's most furious poems, "Cheers, Cheers for Old Cha Cha Ass." While he triumphs retrospectively over his tormentors, the sense of disconnect with his family was even more difficult to exorcise. Whether in his painful level of empathy for the impending divide about to befall a teenager and his working-class parents ("On Seeing One's Self, Years Later, in an Inexpensive Restaurant") or the tears he sheds as his train pulls away, leaving his mother and father behind ("Christmas on Long Island, 1977"), Walta writes sensitively across both books about difficult family relationships. If, in the end, they were

> *mysteries to each other, the butcher, the seamstress, the poet*
> "Visitations and Mortality"

that does not seem to be from any lack on Walta's part of trying to understand their dynamic.

One of Walta's most prominent sources of sustenance during a clearly painful youth was his deep identification with female performers.

> *Drag queens, flowers, and women*
> *who sing are still the fulcrum*
> *of my teeter-totter.*
> "For John Wieners"

he wrote in a late poem, and given that he changed the spelling of his given first name in order to more closely imitate Barbra Streisand, this should come as no surprise. Walta's

> *un-*
> *official high school breakdown*

in which he

> *listened over and*
> *over to Barbra Streisand's first two albums…*
> *…insisting later they alone had saved my*
> *life*
> "Fragrances & Carcinogens"

presaged a lifelong obsession, reflected in his poetry, with (as Michael Bronski calls it in his afterword to this book) "the emotional female voice." From Streisand, Judy Garland, and Barbara Cook to Mariah Carey, Madonna, and Gogi Grant, women with powerful voices and personas parade through his poems. The poetic monologue of his extraordinary "I am not Billie Holiday but I look good in my dress & my running shoes" serves as visceral testament to why so many gay men have taken strength, and needed to take strength, from women who

smoke cigarettes & sing against midnight.

Political History

Leaving Patchogue for his
late 60s campus adolescence
"Visitation & Mortality"

during a time of ongoing national and global ferment, Walta ultimately emerged into the moment of Gay Liberation. The period directly post-Stonewall saw an explosion of political and social organizing in major cities, but also saw the expansion of more open gay cultural production. From *Sebastian Quill* and *Manroot* in San Francisco to *Mouth of the Dragon* and *Christopher Street* in New York to anthologies from Crossing Press (*The Male Muse*) and Gay Sunshine (*Angels of the Lyre* and *Orgasms of Light*), multiple venues emerged for gay poetry. Walta participated in the Boston-based radical collective Fag Rag, founded by Charley Shively, and its publishing offshoot, Good Gay Poets. The press began by publishing John Wieners in 1972; its last book was *Sexually Dangerous Poet* in 1984. Walta became part of a vibrant community of poets in and around Boston: David Eberly, Salvatore Farinella, Freddie Greenfield, Rudy Kikel, Pat Kuras, Ron Schreiber, David Emerson Smith. By the time he was publishing regularly in the later 1970s, poets were exploring all facets of gay identity. Living in a society that largely refused to acknowledge gay relationships, community, or history, he became adept at locating and resurfacing the hidden and the suppressed.

Set in New Hampshire, a pair of poems at the center of *Sexually Dangerous Poet* contrasts this prior repression with the new and momentous openness to which Walta and others were committed. His meeting with

the ghost

of a gay man who never knew love

shifts the connotations of the state motto from the Revolutionary War to a different kind of necessary revolution. The ghost guides him to see bottled gentian in a country meadow; mimicking the position of so many gay men stifled by their society, its flowers are

genetically programmed

never to open.

"Live Free or Die"

On the opposing page, Walta's presence in the state leads to epic destruction, from blight to hurricanes to the maiming of hunter's dogs,

all because

there's a faggot in New Hampshire.

"Power of One"

In this satire of straight society's fears and his other politicized poems, Walta heralds a new generation of publicly gay men not content to remain hidden.

His work in this mode avoids the fate of so much political poetry that collapses into rhetoric. Even when underpinned by anger—as when focused on gay bashing ("Some of Us Wear Pink Triangles"), the suppression of gay artistic history ("Frank O'Hara Homage at Harvard"), or connections between the emerging Moral Majority and previous anti-gay hatred ("It's Earth Wars Worry Me")—he is not yelling at his audience. Where others shout their slogans, Walta employs irony, understatement, even quiet humor. For their subtlety, though, these poems are no less determined to address and correct injustice.

Community History

By the time of Walta's second collection in 1994, *Lingering in a Silk Shirt*, AIDS had been the dominant medical, social, and political reality of gay life for more than a decade. Despite this, *Lingering*'s poems mention AIDS only infrequently until its final section. Among other themes, Walta includes poems of family history ("Driving the Stake Through My Father's Heart," "Twins," "There are no snapshots of my mother"), the language of flowers ("Serious Irises," "Garden Mystery"), and social protest ("Sleep and Trust," "New Brunswick," or, on the campier side, an opera diva's response to censorship in "For Tipper Gore"). Whatever the subject, a sense of conclusion and elegy permeates the poems. Walta vows not to

> spend energy wishing things
> were otherwise
> > "Diagnosis"

but instead of reflecting his present, many poems turn to memories. A new motorcycle reminds him of youthful sex

> down on the sawdust on the
> motor oil
> > "Propriety"

following rides with a friend. Cigarette smoke resurrects a specific ménage-a-trois amid a cascade of scent memories ("Fragrances and Carcinogens"). The destruction of his 1950s childhood home evokes the loss of post-war American hopefulness ("Eminent Domain"). The death of a friend unleashes a haze of recollections linked to college events ("For Carl Wittman"). Knowing the future was short, Walta frequently found himself reckoning with his past.

These poems represent the position of so many gay men of the AIDS generation, forced to come to terms with their mortality, to make peace—or not—with family, to reach an understanding of the import of their experiences and relationships, all at lightning speed. Although highly individual and allied to specific events in Walta's life, they reflect his community's larger experience, its ongoing history. The more direct AIDS poems equally perform this work. They record the ritual of funeral services that skirt the deceased's sexuality and cause of death ("When Jim Died"). They chronicle the greed and duplicity of family members

> *defying your will trying to*
> *have you declared insane, adding*
> *you were trying to go straight*
> "Talking to Jim"

They detail the mental strain of the body

> *suddenly considered*
> *a lethal weapon*
> "The Mouth Poem"

and the physical strain of Kaposi's sarcoma, diarrhea, neuropathy, and exhaustion.

And yet, they also display the great reservoirs of strength that gay men retained in the face of adversity and death. Walta expresses some of this strength in fury, imagining the attention that AIDS deaths would receive if only they befell the most famous celebrities ("Transition in *Newsweek*"). He expresses some of it in love and lust, as with the lengthy sequence "The J. Poems," where he allows himself to

> *muster*
> *romance in the face of*
> *HIV infection*

for a handsome new friend, despite

> *several years of*
> *moving in a haze and getting*
> *silly over no one*
>
> "I Know Your Name"

He expresses some of it in defiance, as when:

> *They tell us repeatedly that the*
> *deadly virus is invariably fatal*
> *Yet every morning, drugged and*
> *insomniac, queers filled with*
> *toxicity and enchantment, fire*
> *and fungus hear their voices,*
> *then broadcast our own news.*
>
> "virus cutting"

There is grief and trauma inherent in Walta telling his community's history—our community's history—both before and after the onset of AIDS. But it is this strength, expressed in anger and tenderness, lust and humor, hope and solidarity, that remains most firmly in memory, as

> *With losses unremembered,*
> *with contributions masked…*
> *…We rise We rise*
> *We rise.*
>
> "It's Earth Wars Worry Me"

Sexually Dangerous Poet

(1984)

Cheers, Cheers for Old Cha Cha Ass

Cheers, cheers for old Patchogue High;
You bring the whiskey, I'll bring the rye;
When we yell   We yell like hell

Acne, puberty, dry heaves each pre-
school morning were not bad enough:

At Patchogue High a circle of charming
boys called me *Cha Cha Ass Borawski.*

Hey, look at Walter, he cha chas when he walks.
He cha chas when he tries to hit a ball.
He probably cha chas while he shits: Let's watch.

(I'm in a toilet stall, making up god.
                    O lord god let me
                    kiss your boot do you
                    think you could
                    disguise me?)

Hey, look, Jayne Mansfield's in Borawski's gym suit.
Hey, Jayne, what's happened to your tits?
If Walter had Mansfield's tits I'd screw him.
If Walter had Mansfield's tits we'd ALL screw him.

Ha ha ha. Cha cha cha. Ha ha Ha Cha
Cha cha   Until

shots called are one's own shots
they are ugly, & must be muffled.

I said *No* to their tenth year reunion,
I added a sketch, I threw in a poem:

Cha Cha Ass Borawski will not be there.
He don't mind the name anymore. He's

thinking of legally adopting it. It's
his only legal thought these days. But

now he meringues when he walks, he
dreams up the devil while he shits.

Trying to Write a Love Poem

for M. Bronski

Since most of my words go to describe
loves that fail, tricks who come & go,
it's no surprise I have no poems for you.

Shall I, trying to write one, say: You
are the man who stole white lilacs from
Harvard to help me find spring in a

dull season? Or that three years ago we
met in a bath house in New York City, strangers
making love in the shelter of sauna & steam?

Would it be too silly to say I like to think
we're Leonard & Virginia Woolf? Don't worry—
I'll not tell which of us is Virginia. But

if I suffer a total breakdown after trying
to write you this poem—& if you
drop all work on your next essay to

put me together, take care of my cat, they'll
know. Meanwhile, *you* should know that
when I see aged couples clutching each

other, walking quick as they can from

muggers & death—I see us. & that if you
die first, someone will have to, like they

would a cat without hope or home, put me to
as it's sometimes called, sleep; & though you
don't believe in heaven, & taught me how empty

& odd my own plan for it was, I imagine we've
already known it—at the baths, in your
loft bed; in stolen lilacs, in each stroke you

give my cat, my cock; & though I'm agnostic
now, I never question why the archangel who
sent down the devil is called Saint Michael.

Wool-gathering

We let go. We
go so far, & then
we let go. I
see it in the way I
stay up long after
Michael's gone to
bed; hear it
in silences
between
what my mother
says & I think
over the long-
distance phone.

My cat died, turned
hard. When Terry
kisses I'm first
to pull away. Stephen
outstares me, everyone
outstays. I am first,
after Neil, to say
Goodnight. And he's
getting set to say
Goodbye.

        Michael
moans in his sleep, throws
arms childlike: out,

trusting. If I could match
the stance, answer
the invitation! But I'm
inside, only smoke
from my cigarettes
gets out. I caress
my poems, proof I
go on. I

make the barriers now, I
avert the eyes. Bruce goes
far as he can without
kissing me. Others go
that far. Others,
further. When Peter says
Shucks as we separate
for night, I know
what he means. And I want
to hold him, I want
to hold on. I want those
funky sounds of first-time
love. I want echoes that
resound, friendship that
makes it make sense, brings
it forward, makes it
continue. I

cover my eyes, forget
my heart, ignore my
cock with its strange
life of its own. But

my mind goes on: white
heat lights each cigarette.

I went to see a doctor once
about it. She said;
"Long as you have Michael,
long as you can sleep, wake
up, you got it good. But if
it goes feel free
to come see me again." I

feel free sometimes, not with her, but
at the ocean, &
over & over in Michael's
arms, in Terry's
eyes, & sitting up
all night long with
Peter. Yet
I know hunger no house meal
satisfies.

> *We let go. We*
> *go so far, & then*
> *we let go.*

For Michael, on the brink of depression & war.

How long will we be allowed
14 windows onto Harvard land?
How long will we afford
five rooms to roam in?
How long to tote around
the great books, the dyke/faggot muses?
How long to care for two cats,
pregnant guppies, dying plants,
each other?

Howling winds shake 14 windows,
the moon rises full each night,
even a snowless winter requires
kisses, my movements
restrict themselves as if already
I inhabited smaller space. Whatever
the quality of life diminishes to I
am your lover, we are our home.

The Autobiographies of Utensils

When it comes to loving I am
a colander. You
can pour your water
all over me, you'll
drain my noodles but
your love will
disappear.
              And the butter of your love,
another story,
              will
              drip
through my aluminum or
ceramic sides, get lost
in the sink.

You don't want it!

When it comes to loving you are
an omelette pan, seasoned & trust-
worthy. You warm evenly,
don't get stuck

(No title)

English was only a second
language, never second nature
to my maternal grandfather He

would shout the heavy
fragments of sentence:
Money! Under! Mattress!

He didn't trust banks, he
knew that here in America
we hide things. When I

was 15 he wanted to see me
with my pants down   I took
them   off   in his toolshed

He ran his fingertips across
my pubic hair & said
Ah! Moustache! That year

he died & I began
looking for other men who'd
take his sort of interest

but it's never been the same
with proper sentences

Christmas on Long Island, 1977

1. *A Private Box on the L.I.R.R.*

He is a poet. He travels through
Patchogue with chocolates from
Switzerland; savors
each triangular bit
as he laughs at
                rectangular worlds.

2. *Visited Grandma's Grave*

Mother calls her Mama—
"Haven't been here," she says,
"since *you* moved away."
                But someone has; left
perky plastic poinsettias, a careful
albeit tasteless
            bouquet;

"Must be the Still girls,"
              says Mother, who
calls anyone under sixty
                "kid"—
"they always loved Mama."

3. *Pygmalion, L.I.*

This poem is for Howie, who told me
I've a lovely ass, & fine-featured
face, then stood me in front of a
full-length mirror to say:

"Now look at your pants—they're
very New York, sure, but
they don't show your body;
& this shirt—great
plaid, but
with that hairy chest you
should always have at least
three buttons doing
absolutely nothing—even in
this weather. Those longjohns
have to go! Now
look at this hair—too much of it,
& *Loving Care* could color that gray;
never say *dye*, it's got
bad connotations. That beard—that
beard! I feel a fine face
under it—no wrinkles at all; just
a moustache would do you fine.
The glasses are awful—but
what glasses aren't? Have you
tried contacts?"

                    This poem
is for Howie, who showed me

his cat Rebekah, though he
had to run through nine rooms
naked to find her—past his
mother, sixty-six & asleep somewhere
in that split-level home.
                              Howie,
who cuts hair for his living &
has lived on Long Island too long.

   4. *Waving*

Train left station; she was
waving at all the windows, so
was my father—though I
had asked them, for my sake,
to leave; the windows
were filthy, not to be
seen through; my face
was clean, showing
                        . visit fatigue.
Stupid, I figured
                        they'd left
simply because I wanted it. But
the train pulled out, leaving
familiar forms. I found
clearer windows, saw her
waving; him too, me—
                              gone already;
they waved at the next car down.

Back in my seat, almost invisible
by contrast; unknown to
other passengers; special
back there only; here, finally,
free, weeping—

On Seeing One's Self, Years Later, in an Inexpensive Restaurant

You study! You pass! You show them you can do it!

Your father talks like
my father, so I change my seat
at the Friendly Eatery I
want to watch you. He

is wearing, your father, one
of those jackets that says
his name is Tony & has
a map of Japan on the
back. I suspect your
mother's been keeping it
clean & pressed since
World War II. She

wears a worn grey sweater I
can't see her skirt. Sometimes
women of the educated
classes dress like your
mother to be comfortable.
Sometimes men of the educated
classes dress like your
father for sportswatching
or fishing trips. But they do not

wear these clothes for pre-

graduation dinners nor do they
slap each other's tired fabric.
Even so, you yourself, long-
haired & high schooley in your
tired, unfashionable clothes,
do not look happy. You look out
the window when there is silence
at your table, just like
other people. Your mother

has long dark wavy hair,
she shakes it & looks out
too I wish I could see her
face maybe she is my mother &
maybe your father, bringing
the pizza back to the counter to
demand more oil is my father, though
he never took us out even for
pizza, & he served in Germany.

Don't study! Don't pass! Don't show them!
I want to say, it will take you years
before or maybe you will never again
enjoy pizza with your folks if you do.

Role Model

Father says I should try harder to be
more like Rory Calhoun I still intend

to be Elizabeth Taylor. Though Mother has
never fully forgiven her—even after the

near-fatal tracheotomy—for stealing
Eddie Fisher from Debbie Reynolds I imagine

myself in violet dresses with violet contact
lenses & the largest diamonds outside the

Tower of London, jewelry box to that other,
lesser, Liz. I too would toss 39 carats

like a stereotypical cheerleader her steady's
class ring: loosely, on a vulgar chain: tick

tock: expensive pendulum as I pass by, ogled:
heavily insured. They would say I'm too fat.

I'd say: *So what's Twiggy's last name?* I'd
keep frightfully well-framed renderings of

my seven husbands, hard-ons, nude on
the piano Barbara Cook would giggle when she

came round to sing songs they'd never let me

record simply because my voice could not

possibly match my face. Even my pets would be
exotic: ocelots, unchained tigers, talking

birds with vocabularies unexpectedly salty as
my own: for what is fantasy but the stroke of

fate, of face, that leaves one person taking
orders in a pizza joint—another—a queen.

My Mother Was a Seamstress

& when we went for Sunday drives
Dad would condescend to drive us
rainy Sundays his golf game gone soggy

I'd content myself back seat solo with a picnic
basket: in it my coloring books & my regular books,
a stuffed monkey crayons & marking pens,

the paper pencil-box I referred to as my
travelling set, all kept secure
in what I insisted was my sewing-box.

I don't care if I kill the three of us
Dad sure hated these drives, & Mother
would turn up the radio, knew all the songs,

sang loud as she had to. I'd hide in the
sewing-box, between the crayons, prop the monkey
in my place, say: *You take it! I won't!*

If you draw me make me purple & red
put me in a kaftan reclined on a bed
Madame Recamier or naked if you've

a sense for miniatures an El Greco cartoon
would be divine. Exaggerate the ear-ring,
eliminate the socks somewhere in the picture
I want my sewing box.

From a Winter's Notebook

11 November 1980

           He's always using
that mouth. If he isn't smoking he's drinking if he
isn't he's talking if he's not he's humming along

or making faces but all with his
mouth, he's making mouths. God he must be
good in bed: I twitch just to look at

that mouth.

30 November 1980

           He was the son of a butcher but he
talked Foucault in living rooms with art on the walls.
When he smoked cigarettes he wondered, *Am I killing*

the Intellectual or the Working Class? Am I

killing the homosexual? *Christians, Cigarettes*
           Placebos.

1 December 1980

Bob says my hair's too long for me

to be sexually attractive. Donny doesn't say that but

when I turned around he said: With that beret and
those long grey curls coming from underneath from the back you
could pass for 45.

Michael loves me with short or long hair. My mother doesn't.
If I visit her during Christmas & my hair's still
this long
it will ruin her holiday. If I stay here to hide the fact
it is so long that will ruin her holiday too. If I corn-row

my curls that will be politically incorrect. If I put it
under a Rootie Kazootie cap discerning queens will say:

How tired! Early Barbra drag.

1 December 1980

His mother had taken to
synthetic fabrics *Everything must be
washable* But he remembers a time when she

wore chiffon and lace, dresses with impractical buttons
Such a nuisance! He'd help her how he loved
those phony gleams: black plastic onyx,

        paste diamonds plastic
        mother of pearl—

She made rags of the fabric but she saved

the rags & the buttons deep in a box they still
wink at him on visits home while she sits

stiffly in a chair *In & out of the machine,*
she says, *Every time, looks like new. Feel it.*

He doesn't like to feel it, he prefers
remembering her in flowered silk, fingering
for bargains when there were   bargains

8 December 1980

Michael said that hearing Tova
play cello from the next room reminded him of a
Bergman film, but Walta as he watched her
in the same room his room that night of rehearsal
thought the French or English directors might better

depict the scene: the familiar art & book-lined
room, with Tova in a straight-backed chair brought
in from the kitchen, playing what sounded to his ears
classical but turned out to be impromptu. How

did she do this? How many centuries of music flowed
through her head to produce these sounds? And was it

semi-surreal to him because she is a woman, and
in his room? If Donny played cello & played it

in his room would it still have resembled a movie?

27 January 1981

              Did he ever truly honor his
feelings, or did he sort of humor them? He never danced
them to death, like Electra; but almost dead. He hadn't

trusted his face for years now. Once he feared it was too
naked, now he knew there were all these costumes he
hadn't bought, & wouldn't recognize.

                          No meeting ground,
he worried. Alison was at the door in a new coat,
wanting to be reassured. And he said he deplored
the buttons! *Too brassy!* he said: but did he mean
Alison's barging into his afternoon-with-book; or
his own behavior? Was it not hostile, these defenses
mercilessly laid up in reserve for minor invasions?

                The buttons *were* brassy, but this
was no reason to snap so. *Maybe they'll tarnish*, said
Michael. How had Michael stood him all these years?
The buttons were muted & tasteful, next to him.

27 January 1981

              He was annoyed Bruce didn't
drop in more often but he never climbed the stairs
to Bruce. On the landing they shared he left notes,

he left gifts. At dinner at mutual friend Terry's he'd
drop: Haven't seen Bruce for *days*: annoyed. And yet who

was more reclusive than he? Garbo didn't count—
no one he knew knew her story—but in his circle
several knew more than enough of his.

11 March 1981

It is a serene landscape,
colorless & sprawling. From the bend in the
river to the straightness of the highway, all his

but for now & then runners. How he loves to pretend
it's England, walking along with a borrowed dog. Were he

totally alone he might feel he'd no reason to be there.
He needs reasons to be places, he doesn't "hang out."

He enjoys walking to and from work because
the direction is questionless. But

on weekends he can't get himself out of the house unless
it's for shopping trips planned in advance. He'll buy
records & flowers but he won't go looking

for a sexual partner, that's too vague. He'd
like to know if someone stopped him
—a cop; his mother—
he'd be able to tell the errand—
& be allowed to go on with it.

St. Theresa of Hemenway Street

for Terry Tobin

St. Theresa of Hemenway goes
down to the co-op, buys
vegetables & checks out
men. St. Theresa's my
sister, we hunt witch
together, prefer diamonds
to souls. *See the diamond*

in my ear? says St. Theresa; I
say: *See the manbone in
mine?* We

go walking. St. Theresa passes
playgrounds, has a boy in one
of them. He thinks he is a
super-hero, he's called
Tyrannosaurus Rex. St. Theresa

worries he's male-identified:
power, largeness, eats his
(almost) vegetarian ma & me. *How*

did this happen, asks St. Theresa,
*with you for his aunt, & his
father gay, too.*

                              Time to picnic,
shouts St. Theresa; lays a
blanket near the Charles, bring
white wine & fried chicken wings:
no vegetarian, St. Theresa today:
We all put flesh in our mouths
in times of plenty.

St. Theresa had a steady lover,
lost him to a law school. Sometimes
the phone rings, he's there, she's
there too: *But in the night,*
says St. Theresa.

To get out of this bummer St. Theresa
plays Simon & Garfunkel, re-
members the Sixties. Men
had longer hair, crooned
Beatle tune titles in her ear;
her bosom buttoned over
With *End-the-war.*

St. Theresa reads
Hemingway, says: *There were*
& are men worse than that. He
had *thirty cats.*

St. Theresa reads night hours
away; with Tyrannosaurus Rex
in bed she can. She plays
jazz records low. Puts out

her light, & cats crawl
up, a lap rug, fur between
fingers for St. Theresa. *It*
may just be cats, she
says, *but it's not*
super-heroes & it's not
going to law school.

St. Theresa has a headache,
says her glasses are
too strong: longs
to see without them, takes
them off, depends on me
to cruise the runners: *The ones*
in white shorts, when sweat
makes men see-through...

St. Theresa says there's too much
distance: between: friends: between
smiles on the street; between men who
love you all night & stay in
the morning for coffee
& cranberry buns. St. Theresa
looks at the river, says:
What would we do if it would not flow?

After Doing Coke at Steve's Goodbye Party

Two week old white spider chrysanthemums
no breezeway on the house Mother always

regretted that but blue slates descended
from kitchen door to rock garden back

yard the smell of Cities Service gas
station & chrysanthemums not spider

but sturdier, shorter & by time they
bloomed it was too late to sit cross-

legged near them Mother didn't work
or leave the house she'd watch out

the back windows & say Walter you'll
catch your death Get off that grass

Come home & live with me she says now
but snorting coke in her memory-insulated

attic is hardly incentive for
doing that though of course it would

help: She'd be on Scotch & we'd both
be hyper & silent at intervals, separately

going off to the kitchen sink cupboard or
the mattress with the teddybear amidst

Mousketeer books to gather flowers
we'd come back to each other with flowers,

flushed faces   flowers   the sturdy smells
of transformed petals

Valentine's Day 1981

A cannister of chocolate kisses
with Asians in black red & gold:
all those kisses! In Hershey Pennsylvania

I've been told even streetlamps look
like chocolate kisses the streetwalkers
lick the poles look how erect they

stand in moonlight leaning against
each other *How erect they stand*
in moonlight leaning against each other.

We stare across the table, drinking
Colombian coffee & talking about
El Salvador Neither of us has

had much love lately We've been
buying records, expensively tinned
candied mints Individually wrapped

Three Poems from the Pompeii Exhibit

for Greg Parks

Cicada in Rock Crystal

It is little, oblong, & very clear.
It stopped living long ago. *Right*
now I want you: I'm odd, long, &
sounding loudly.

               You look
at the Labors of Hercules
in relief, on a silver bowl.
Naked men chasing each other
out in the open, *out in the open!*
nineteen hundred years ago.
"What a coffee cup it'd make,"
you say, *"What a thing*
to rub your fingers against
first thing in the morning."

I know no relief, I don't live
on a silver bowl. I'll not keep
this secret for hundreds of years
or even this odd spring season. I
rub my leg backs together, & every-
where you run you'll hear cicada

31

cracking through crystal: no rock
crystal encases the shrill call
of my need, no museum houses
my whore's voice yet.

Priapus Past & Present

At the Boston Museum there's a flying penis
made of shiny bronze—black, & looking heavy
under glass.
   Three bells hang below it; no sound
ejaculates now.

"Bronze tintinnabulum with three hanging bells,"
says the plastic card beneath. We're museum-
goers, we move on.
    "Flying fuck, with tinkle,"
is on my tongue, but
there's a kid at my elbow, another
at my knee, & their father's
already pushing them quickly
past the fossil facts of life.

In the same glass case, but made of clay,
is *"Dwarf Reading"*—a stern little man, bearded,
burdened with a penis long as he is tall.

Burdened, I said, knowing the weight of a small one.

The dwarf rides nowhere. Nineteen hundred years ago
ash came down, left him & his big earthen prick
museum pieces.

       In a cold city, in
asexual museum air, we
get to see them, for a buck-seventy-five, as
they were: driven nowhere on lust, flying
with silent bells.

       You're
not made of bronze, though you picked up sun somewhere,
& glow to me.
       I
don't know if you have three bells, but I
mean to ring the ones I find. I
don't want it to be long as you are tall,
I know the length of a short one, inside.

Yet, for a simple plastic label, care-
fully worded to tell me you want me, I'd
shove all these relics aside, sit on you
under glass lest ash fall down again, & plastic cards
tell other people different things
in a warm city, hundreds of years from now.

Rehearsing for a Satyr Play

On the museum wall a woman
crouches doglike before

her lover. It's Pompeii,
these things

happened. *"You'd think*

they'd hang it above
the heads of children,"

says a lady braving
inner-city Boston
for the sake of
this exhibit.

       I push
my ash against
your Priapus; am glad
to be flesh, not a
fresco: We lose
interest in history
& art, go home
with only that
woman's pose
in mind.

Aborted Adonis

for Bruce Goodchild

Waking in a storm, pre-night
dark, thinking
             I could run. I

find my jock, my
shoes; push floor,

    sit up,
see the cactus blooming
on the sill.
How
nice. Naked buttocks
kiss wood, press hair;
press the door frame,
it flows, the force

reminds.
             Beginning again
to clothe my body, put
limbs in shorts & shirt & hooded
jacket, *can't ride*
without a helmet,

                    & I'm
                down
      the
stairs
        searching for keys,
safety-
pinned; they'll
kill me one day

coming unpinned.
I lose my wind,

don't find it. Fault
the storm, the
steps. I climb,
do not undress,

do not fly.

Normal as Two Ships in the Night

for Alison Pirie

After a while, in the larger cities, we
do not talk or think of normal. The young
student, blond, clipped, whistling

the allegro of Sibelius' violin concerto
is not normal; his lips
are too tight, his soul

is not in this frenetic tooting,
only his fear, flared-up, it is

his lighthouse & his horn as we pass self
to self in Harvard Yard. We pass quickly

in Harvard Yard, I am hiding in the dark
funk of a Laura Nyro tune, we know we're

incompatible, but grateful we will
probably not mug or harm or murder

but unknowing, imagining, we pass

quickly in Harvard Yard, in Harvard
Square, in Copley Plaza, in America

we do not talk of normal, we whistle
odd snatches of song, violent passions
composed for solo instruments.

bez tyutu*

I move through crowds un-
noticed, even in my
black cape, jewels
clasped at the nape
of my neck: scape-
goat diamonds.
I think
my skin
    transparent,
think my thoughts
dreams: crystal balloons,

& they float, & I go by,
unnoticed. Would you

be fooled, if I tiptoed
or danced within reach—
if I was not twirling,
or flying with the help
of strings or would

you put out a hand
to stop my crazy motion?

*Polish: *untitled.*

Gentility

for David Roberts

A large woman on Fifth Avenue, im-
patient with the hot dog man catering

to her & to her grandchildren points him
to me, says: *There's a gentleman behind*

you, waiting to be served. At the corner

of Lenox Av & 116th Street a young woman
waits with me until a bus comes to

remove me from

her neighborhood. In Central Park
an androgynous figure in clown suit

alternately crawls for change & dances
blithely before cross-town cars,

assuming
they'll stop.

29 May 79
New York City

Traveling in the Wrong Century

for Joan Doyle

Hotels we stay in
have no flowers left by management,
we manage without
writing tables set discreetly
off-lobby; no chandeliers
cast dancing rainbows 'cross
our faces as our feet
take rich baby steps
into deep carpet. There are no
potted palms, no old world
charm, no bell boys, damn
near no fantasy. If shoes
are left in the hall they're
polished off by morning.

Power of One

I am the sole homosexual
in Wilton, New Hampshire, & I

was imported only this afternoon.
Rafts of whirligigs scatter

as I approach by canoe: cut-
worms devour potatoes,

raccoons split wood houses,
scoop, eat, birds inside,

are hunted & shot in turn
by shadowed dogs, & hunters.

Mining insects leave striations
'cross leaves of water lilies,

beavers topple trees, water
rises, raises mosquitoes, fleas.

Grey, white, black, yellow
birches dwarf blueberries;

no safe spot, no refrain. Hurri-
cane David yanks branches

from fruit trees, Japanese

beetles make lettuce artless lace,

porcupines pierce the tongues
of hunters' dogs—all because

there's a faggot in New Hampshire.

Live Free or Die

Here in New Hampshire the ghost
of a gay man who never knew love

stops me in the meadow, leads me
by web-chain to his lean-to, rot

& mice dung. Points to my penis,
wants me to piss on his rusted

bed springs, lay naked down on
wet coils.

My own bed has its own stains.
Spotless he walks before me,

points out the *bottled gentian*:
not poisonous, but purplish-blue,

lovelier than Venetian glass;

genetically programmed
never to open.

Travel Fatigue #2

for Orolin John

On the way to lovers
we drove thru Cincinnati,

Arkansas & Stockholm.

On the way cars
broke down, tears

shattered windshield.

On the way Debussy
brought clouds

from notes, & lovers

left us. On the
way to lovers

we paid toll,

tires flattened, & we found
even air costs money.

On the way to lovers
we became landscape

resembling tv shows;

we stole books
to repair engines,

lost looks, lost
motor oil, love became

expensive, travel

ridiculous. On the way
to lovers the radio

crackled country,
western, Ravi Shankar,

opera, Streisand, jazz

ways to ride on
waves without & during

love. On the way
to lovers we found

substitutes, refreshment
stands, endless

repetition.

Tired Song-&-Dance Act

Tired of promiscuity,
tired of abstinence,
tired of the presence,
of the absence.

I'm wearing my black
bandana: on my head:
central; symbolizing:
too queenie for you!

Don't touch me, I'm
tired, dancing
in the market
for a one-to-one man.

My Perfect Poetry Reading

In my head a famous poet
Arrives places. Handsome graduate students
greet him at gangplanks settle him in

snazzy hotel rooms. *Can you be comfortable,*
Sir, Is there anything more I
can do for you?

They've always called ahead to ask my mother
my favorite food: lobster lobster in salads
lobster they crack the shells they'd cook

them themselves they dip chunks in
butter laced with garlic
                          Is there anything more?

Disregarding garlic breath they kiss me they unfold
beds to ascertain second sheets
were not forgotten
                    they pull down the shades
                    on borrowed windows unless
                    I say I love the view

They escort me to the reading they announce me
lovingly awkwardly, for that's how I love
them best: all lips & feet & verbal confusion

I do my act for them my college

educated working class paid-for mouth I
get paid enormously for these displays

of ego & after another dinner they
take me back
       I hear you drink cognac,
       I hear you blow dope, I sip

& I suck with them: intake time we sit
cross-legged on the floor 'til our joints
loosen up they'll never forget, they say
anally penetrating a living legend

Some of Us Are Stretched Tighter Than Others

He says all the birds are flying
south this year, & I

am too intense to sleep with.
It's warmer, that's why they

go, kissing me is
kissing February, it stretches you

out & then sticks in the tongue,
the icicle tongue.

              I
only wanted warmth myself,
didn't feel like flying

for it; & these eyes—
my mother's side of the family

has them. These feathers—
how I've plucked for them!
And you
want things easy, you

want to fly without
greasing up the engine,
without

twisting up the rubber
band.

God, the unplucked notes.

1.

He brought me here, told me to love
no one. I complied. He told me

to remove my clothes, & often
kneel, I'm still

naked on my knees.

        He told me
to open wide, catch flies—

I'm full now, wings
flap in my stomach;
the oddest songs
escape me.

2.

& so you don't find me
sexually attractive. I sit

I wait for your mind-change.
I have this alternative:

changing my own mind,

not finding *you*

attractive. I've tried this—

I've tried changing tires;
I've tried suicide.

3.

In an ideal society
John would not love me, he'd

be turned on to someone
who'd see him & dance

steps leading
each to each. In an

ideal society I'd have seen
the signs: DANGER—
                      DON'T WALK—
                      DEAF CHILDREN—

We are here. It is no
ideal society, I've seen you

& I want —; *I want*

        (Never to know
        never to know

never to know

your body. I'm
not good at it.)

In an ideal society I'd suck
those big, glorious nipples;

open your green button fly, my
teeth not tired by
biting words. How I'd

give you head
in an ideal society.

4.

He brought me here, he told me
to love no one. I lied. I've

never tried naked
never tried *tied*, but

here, from this leash, leather
or irises I extend to you

this improbable connection

until we touch
I itch

5.

Notice how this first icy rain
makes these twigs glisten, *so*

snap-able. Like wire I

stretch out before you, not about
to break but put across

your resonant chest how
I'd play with you—
melodies!—

Denied here, I sit
patient, silent;
there is no symphony
from unplucked notes.

9-13 Nov. 79
Cambridge

Direct or Indirect Rebound Tenderness

for Jim Gleason

It is not when you poke me that hurts,
rather when you

take your fingers away
& where they were

      or inches beyond,
within, bowels start throbbing.

And it is like that
  when you put on
your knit hat, you unravel me.
It is not

the gesture itself: hand holding hat,
down motion, *it's on*, but

that the hat's the final thing I see
leaves me
bruised again, *invisibly*.

Surprising Kisses

for Malcolm

You were my first S&M man, you
showed me the ropes, though we
had to imagine them, in the dorm
at the St. Mark's Baths.

      Don't move
one wrist from the other, you
ordered, *Now lick me all over.*

      And like a tired
or drunken ballet dancer my tongue
twirled, passion without form,
taking your pleasure moans for
applause, & flowers.

        Now & then
I'd *plié* at your closed
mouth, lick your clipped beard &
tight lips;
      now & then, on cues
very much your own you'd
open your mouth, & give mine
surprising kisses: How odd,
how more desirable these
than those given freely,

in uncategorized love, as if kisses
are just commodities, obeying
the law of supply & demand.

                                    Later you
worried that my hair, wet all the while
from whirlpool & sauna, steambath & love-
sweat, would catch me cold. You offered me
taxi fare home. Surprising concern,
surprising kisses: But like men of
less choreographed fantasy you
said *Goodbye*, & *Good knowing you*, & I

danced uptown unbound.

Hunger

Paralyzed in heat
the man stroking
his cock does not
see the toilet door
is open, or men
entering, not
entering; he
dream-strokes;
he's needing
a hole to
come in, a
hole beyond
his fingers but

doors open, doors
close: hasty
steps, none
toward him.

The man is not *my type*.
He is no pirate. He is
no hippyhunk, bearded
& bandana-ed. He is not
a hard hat on his lunch
break. He is not well-
contoured, there is no
color come-on in his
clothes. I go to my

knees before him, he
does not notice until
contact, wet lips
wake him, partly,

& he comes, giving
in, giving his
extraordinary
hunger to me.

Sociologically Challenged

I have a hard cock, you
have a hard cock, *every-*
thing else is broken How
the parts howl at us. We

will not reach each other's
hard-ons : *broken eyeballs*
                broken grasps;

We will not hear each
other's lips smack

 : *broken ear-drums*
  broken thoughts.

If we could crawl—
 but we can't—

If we could grunt—

If we believed in
each other's ass holes—
mouths—finger stumps—

Numb to altruism & even
sex we roll
individually

onto our stomachs & we

push & we pull & we
imagine the other, or
another
*   & we come: You come,*
*   I come—*

semen might have
calmed our cuts & sore spots

—How they howl at us!
from our stomachs,
from the hard wood floor.

For Emily Dickinson & Charley Shively:

I saw two men—and wanted both—
but neither—wanted me—
and that—is the extent—of my—
Promiscuity.

Perversity

I know my holding onto
a book of poems by Ezra Pound
separates Sylvia Plath
from Adrienne Rich
on one shelf in America
but I keep it there.

I know my lust feelings
for my lover's boyfriend
are illicit—not even smart;
but I do like the man, I do
like the man, I do, & I never
was much good at *platonic*.

Many men women & children
would call me, christians
would call me, shrinks &
my mother & right wingers
everywhere would call me
perverse but very likely
for wrong reasons.

Salome

How many times have I wanted to stand
moonlit, my veils damp & tired

his head on a plate, delivered me
from depths of desire & a cistern, slippery

with his blood, *he'd never let me suck it*
while he was alive, & I was

alive, & wanting him. *I want him now,*
I have him now, I kiss him—

Who wouldn't dance
for the death of a man

who will not take you in as you
take him, call his name before him:

Master, Sir, will not kiss you
even when the moon's obscured

by clouds & no one would see
the kiss. How I wanted

his lips on my body; how that body
danced!

Against Sex

for Peter Tenney

If it's followed by depression,
a sense of something missing,
& depression leads to premature
departure,   *why do it?*

If it's going to disco
bars to be   lulled   to be
deafened   to be dulled, do
regimented, fascist steps &
call it *dancing*   *why do it?*

If it's reduced to mundane, fucked-up
masculine matters of   *I put it
in you*   OR   *You put it in me*
            OR
I can do it only with men who
are not fat, not femme, are
professional, have less than
30 years' experience; don't do
drugs, or S&M   *why do it?*

If it's kneeling to married men,
who want cake,   who want to be
eaten: who live *respectable*   but
let queer creeps, commie

faggot   weirdos   blow them
in the dark   *why do it?*

If it's the bringing together
of two with separate politics
(& yet only semen is swapped)
: if the man is   hot   but
works with poison gas, believes
in the future   of nuclear
power, supports a government
in whose eyes   he   is an out-
law, *why do it?*

Warm bed,   shelter-bush,   thirst of mind;
hunger of body   to eat   of its kind;
arms that hold what needs to be held;
fingers that move in, further in; *I*
know why I do it,   hoping always
to once find a *man* who
does not like the word, gropes
for renewal & a new name.

It's Earth Wars Worry Me

1.

Exterminate homosexuals? Walta you are so paranoid!
Blond & young he glared at me

Incredulous. I with no patience to explain
Nazis preceded the American Party for Manhood &

before then & after them & right now Dean
Wycoff the Moral Majority Christians to burn us

as witches. They see us
& with hard-ons tied
between their legs
say *we* should die
for being kinky.

These walls
No apples fall
over them. We
can't make love
here: lights & guns.

2.

Dead faces, gaping holes: history.
Rats in the catacombs: prediction.

3.

MIT's Pi Lambda Phi frat marches through
Harvard Square demanding death for gays:

A Joke, they tell reporters.
There are no accidents, says Andrea.
And there are no jokes,
just straight people.

Anne Frank didn't need a diary, wrote
Charley Shively years ago, *she*
needed a hand grenade.

4.

Archaic Catholics call their
ancestors angels call us
occasions of sin. Our

promiscuous faces our
lascivious eyes invite them
to sin, sin. We are our own

icons We are faggots they want faggots
to burn.

5.

If San Francisco slides into the sea Dean
Wycoff will say it was because so many gay
people were allowed to live there & people
who lose property in that slide will not

want it to happen again. Gays are

expected to let things happen again, the Church
burns us, we rise: Hitler exterminates the gays
of Europe, they rise. With losses unremembered,
with contributions masked *(O Emily was an odd
spinster, Old Walt was a bit weird)* We rise We rise
We rise

If I Ran Harvard University…

The football team the rowing team
all the teams & the men who belong

to private dining clubs would become
the building & grounds crews, only

they'd not get to wear green work
clothes, just jockstraps & collars

& the men who work buildings & grounds now
who understandably mutter as they pick up

refuse of the rich would lord it over
the aforementioned with whips & studded

belts WHACK on those fine white asses
Let's see those wide butts move! & when

their fathers came visiting in limousines
how surprised & secretly pleased they'd be

by their son's marks

I am not Billie Holiday but I look good in my dress & my running shoes.

Sometimes in the living room between the speakers I pretend to be Billie Holiday singing "These Foolish Things Remind Me of You." The song does not take much range, good for me & maybe, by then, why she picked it too. I find it increasingly hard, not being Billie Holiday. No-voiced, I don't know what to do with all these songs.

At other times I am Barbra Streisand. It is an integral part of my survival, why & how I am still here, being now & then, Barbra Streisand. I steel myself up on my heels, I turn chiffon into armor, I send every word of displeasure disappointment & hurt out to counterattack. I'm unable to forgive, today. This works when the stance is enhanced by talent. I cannot sing. I bring borrowed intelligence & fury & phrasing & weight to the words. I am a mimic. But I copy the greats.

The fish tank is comforting. Life has even greater limitations. I commiserate. I leave for work Monday morning but: *Would I stay in a warm bed. Would I prefer being wrapped in arms. Would I choose to be alone over a second cup of tea, a second cigarette?* No one did well at work on Monday. The smoking room was filled all morning, the coffee ran out by ten, elongated faces settled in corners: mine too. I was Billie Holiday eight hours ago, I stood alone between the speakers, between inverted obelisk black jet earrings, I smelled the gardenia behind my ear, I felt my silk dress *from the inside*, I felt this rustle, I heard this drum, I moved my notes like a saxophone, like a cello, leave me alone now.

Eleven people were crushed & otherwise battered to death on their way into a rock concert last night, The Who in Cincinnati went on. Where would the energy of 18,000 expectants go if the music, if the show, did not go on? I imagine being on acid, stepped to death, I imagine being part of a crowd, the word *Stop* lost from my vocabulary, the word *Help* beyond my understanding.

When I am making love, when I am having sex & there is pain or there is nonenjoyment or my mood goes from red to dark gray I stop the action, I pull away. I have never had to slap a hand. If I wanted the tit-clamps off, if I wanted symmetrical pain stopped, they were off, it stopped, I continued. In Fenway orgies, fucked suddenly too often, too eagerly, I have pulled my pants up, I have walked away. I have never heard The Who. I love the rhythms of rock & of fucking. I love the abruptness of *Stop*, the potential of *Help*.

On tv last night, a nationwide insidious show called *The 700 Club*, Pat Robertson hiding behind Christ's name subtly strung together homosexuality, black witchcraft and the dismemberment of teenage bodies.

I always wear running shoes, even though boots go better with my leather jacket, sandals better with my flowing shirts. I fear wearing color. I've put my earrings in a soapstone box, I hide that behind books. I consider myself, women & men like me, an endangered species. *Survival* is a word I do not feel cozy with, it has concentration camps on the other side of it. This is why I listen not to The Who, who keep on, after all, rocking, but to Billie Holiday. This is why I smoke cigarettes & sing against midnight & try so very hard to become her.

Indexing Judy Garland's Life: A Found Poem, from Gerald Frank's Bio.

Birth
childhood
stage debut
training
changes name

death of father
early love affairs
drug use
poetry

remarriage of mother
in love with Artie Shaw
romance with David Rose
marriage with Rose
health problems

divorce from Rose
in love with Joe Mankiewicz
psychological problems
psychiatric treatment

weight problem
marriage with Minnelli
birth of Liza
drug dependence

suicide attempts
(pp. 230, 281, 299, 360
402, 427, 525, 534, 541)
suspended by MGM
financial problems
contract terminated

relationship with Luft
separation & divorce from Minnelli
marriage with Luft
birth of Lorna

death of mother
loss of Oscar
birth of Joey
drinking habits
TV debut

conflicts with Luft
reunited
battle of custody of children
illness (overdose) in London
divorce from Luft
quarrel with sisters
TV series

legal problems
marriage with Herron
marriage with Mickey Deans
death
funeral

Sullivan

[August 1971—July 1981]

   Suddenly crippled, dragging his
hind legs about he who sprang
from back stairs to front porch like

Supercat: black, moving thru Rousseau-
like abundance of leaves spookily laced
by green eyes

          He still cleans himself, &
gulps his food. But he pulls those
so recently powerful legs
                angrily

         Begs to die? To live?
           As before?

25 June 81

   If whole cats sleeping chase
rabbits on the run, their

paws aquiver Do crippled cats remember
their flying limbs?

25 June 81

.

       Sullivan fell asleep
I imagined he dreamed he was
not crippled because when he
woke up he tried to sit up
in the old, proud, Egyptian way
& was annoyed he could not
& surprised.

8 July 81

All he knew was that I was
killing him, & that he
had the disadvantage of being crippled, & I
the advantage of chloroform

10 July 81

Things Are Still Sudden & Wonderful

Once it was 1962 & somebody
kissed you you freaked he

held you down pressed his
15-yr.-old football team thighs hard

against yr. thin-kid-with-glasses
legs It was like a Lana Turner movie

; you decided to be gay. In 1982 yr. lover
puts you down on all fours & masturbates

you sometimes you come with a leash on
in more than one room. You've

not forgotten the football player's name

Uncollected Poems

[stick it in sweet man mine]

stick it in sweet man mine
cornhusks are drying my field's overripe
but my man you're here right now so
stick it in me sweet man mine
if trumpets don't blow me i don't care
if stars don't collide what does it matter
if you go away quickly as you come
i'll be ready so
stick it in me sweet man mine
know that the laws of this land mean nothing
to me know that the dreams of my childhood
fell off the sill when i reached fifteen
know that if i cry you won't hear it
if i bleed you won't get stained so
stick it in me sweet man mine
stick it in me sweet man whosoever
stick it in me
stick it in me and
praise the Lord you was born a man

A Harmless Tail

theodora himsuck wanted to be cool
bought a wig to warm his shoulders
stuck plastic lilies here & there
& a patent leather paisley shirt.
this was back in '69 you see

no one looked, so to be heard
Streisand songs all day he'd sing
and in the night, between the acts,
still unheard he'd change his tune;
picked up Dylan, then the Beatles,
tried to go bi for Sonny and Cher;
sang all day between the acts,
lost his windpipes, then decided
to get some drums but couldn't pay
and never did learn how to play

theodora looked around:
hey man, will you hear my sound
but no one was around that day
that night or that year
so theodora sang alone

theodora changed his name:
hippie himsuck, ring it true
(excrement doesn't change the smell;
once a weed a theodora)

temptations passed him everyday:
pills and chills and stainless blades
but theodora chickened out—
nothing is so hard to lose.

theodora bought some diamonds
stuck them smartly in his ears
made believe they weren't rhinestones
stuck a ruby in his navel
made believe it wasn't blood
hung a mirror on his boobies
hobbled in on golden fruit boots
flashing eyes of real mink lashes
that smelled like rats in rain;
smiled at everyone he could
with his lips of balsa wood

tried and tried and tried for cool
but labeled FAGGOT at his school
he found a thing that wouldn't let him down.
it didn't care he wasn't female
it didn't care he wasn't male
it didn't care he had no lover
it let him drip and smile
& left his mother
to worry over Heaven

[For those who arrived too early or too late]

For those who arrived too early or too late
or never will or do not wish to,
it is all right now to pith a frog in public,
to do anything to get to the nerve of things:
drop drawers/show claws/flaunt flaws/fuck
your friend through the asses of his friends.

On the way to work, hostile but carefully dressed,
dressed to kill anyone's potential not to like you
(as your bestsellers on the subway seek approval),
dressed to kill your boss's plan to fire you, you see
a man standing in a tree. Like branches that support him
he is clothed in green. Like a tight-rope dancer he
manages. We stand beneath him, we stand across the street,
we don't want to meet him, we don't want to see him fall;
he is merely our work-bound amusement, and we
envy what appears to be his freedom. Free doom:
Not everyone climbs urban trees on Monday morning.
Briefcases would flip, Pucci ties turn to nooses,
we'd hang like unwanted kittens, and be forgotten.
No one remembers the unattached, and so we cling.
We require mirrors and hooks. We are mirrors and hooks.

Which brings us back to friends:
like mirrors they break, and bring eternities of bad luck;
like hooks they pierce, promise   and pull out.

84

Thanksgiving Weekend, 1976

In this rancid age
when love & butter
are both
prey to cockroaches
I am barraged:

I

This room is strewn with poetry books &
books on Bloomsbury & buried books on
pornographic subjects: self-portraits everywhere,
it must be home to an ego/nympho/maniac.
It is hard, getting thru the 70s, he says.
He is twenty-nine & discontent. He thinks
it isn't that much better than it was at seventeen
or twelve. The dissolution's gained sophistication;
the breakdowns, class. There is a certain finesse
to finishing errors & eras, he says; somewhat erudite.
Sometimes he goes for days not knowing
what he is talking about. Exact meanings
escape him.

II

Late in the afternoon light in his room
turns plant leaves to jade; he's afraid
to leave the house these hours, that
something might rob the transition;

he only sees the room change light
two days a week, leaving it in sun
& finding it in moon the other five.

III

He wonders if the music is too loud
for the sleeper downstairs; he curses
(silently) abrupt crescendos
& unduly large orchestrations.
He thanks the Lord for Ray Charles,
then turns down the volume. Heavenly choirs
depress him, like Christmas
they remind him of something
missing; he's forgotten what.
He's forgotten a lot,
& not, he insists, voluntarily.

IV

Tonight the air smelled of college
though that is miles & years away;
he does not yet know what
to make of time. He says
it's like oatmeal—he's kidding,
of course—nondescript, sometimes
good, never understood, impossible
to appreciate, a truthful friend,
oozing, lumpy, never to be touched
(he goes on for days, a wince
increasing its way across his face

like a caterpillar moustache);
it enters orifices & comes out
eyes or ass, what does it matter
(his oatmeal ramblings? Destination?);
it is all, he concludes, needing spice.

V

He hasn't cooked in weeks, he hasn't
done a watercolor in months; often
feeling without show he
tells friends not to come around;
the mood isn't right, he's a
headache, or the moon's too full.
The flowers are wilted, he objects,
reminiscent of weekend expectation,
representative of weekday discontent.

VI

The cat howls objection to the universe,
finds an evil spirit in the hall:
it must be the moon, or the mirror,
the unsmiling face on the wall.

VII

He is always in search of explanation
but the moon looks so good reflected from
the surface of his green marble head;
he goes no further; it stops
his meditation.

Dead Languages

He didn't remember my name,
this letter-sweatered man
with six hundred & fifty pages
toward his doctoral degree
in long-dead tongues. I
remembered his, I've a knack
for simpler bits of life:
three letters, one syllable,
two vowels, rhymes with bee.
I said it on departure, stung.
He could muster only dusty words,
a prospectus on the day, its
matriculated absence of me.
It was 6:30 a.m., the sky
was showing us a clear trick
or two, without words.

[Relationships have boundaries]

Relationships have boundaries
like discontented countries.
Filled with questions & fear
sentries patrol,
never pleased with travelers' answers.
Visas are granted by mutual need
and unlimited compromise.
I am now quite invisible.
We exist, if at all, in subsequent treaties;
in peace, perhaps we are boring,
in war silenced by guns.

[All in white but loveless & without music]

All in white but loveless & without music
I marched timidly toward the VD clinic.
There were no flowers, no slim red rug;
suspicious green arrows marked the way
from front door down thru crooked corridors.
An old man trying to clean linoleum—
made filthy by feet like mine—growled at me
to move along, & then apologized. I've the
air of confused saints for such situations:
blank-eyed, glowing, in search of fiery stakes.

After assumption by elevator, missing angels,
I faced a desk. On either side, far as sight,
on unfolded folding chairs sat rows of men
looking at each other, and at me—odd place
to meet a friend; germs nor cops can stop us.
I myself need to be alone times like this,
especially when dressed in white, fully aware
of the thinness of veneer; it cannot hide stain.
Sure enough, with two point four million units
of something unromantic shot up my vestigial
vestibule, no virgin could save me, I saw red.

[Harvard has no class these days; nothing does]

Harvard has no class these days; nothing does.
Where are the men in white flannel roadsters
who'd run over regular Cantabrigians
with only a silver toot for comment?
Gone with the goldfish, I suppose.
Harvard men have always been well-fed.
Even today, dressed like everyone else,
their bodies show centuries of breeding,
like horses—those far more useful studs.
Just the other day I met one,
buns worthy of the Busch-Reisinger,
invited him on up into my room
which will someday be a Harvard dorm anyway.
I was just offering a sneak peek;
but he knew his place—and mine,
patted my public school ass with his class ring
& said: Harvard men don't do that.
There was desire in that mitt but
he was in need of a son to continue the myth.

Didn't That Bother You

You pick me up on Anderson Bridge
at three on a Saturday morning; we

have a mutual friend, only I
know him better; I've been cruising

you since I moved here; you never
look back; I blame that on this

being New England, not New York.
Now we talk about

teeth, & smiles.   You suggest we
move deeper into shadow.   You

ask what I do for a living in
the same tone you tell me to

sit on your lap. You pull down
my sweatpants, say it's sick

to wear a jock. I tell you
it's nothing to do with

respectability. Someone
slides in on the shadow

to see how it snaps. You

pull me away

as if he were a cop, or I
your very own. *Didn't that*

bother you? you ask, *he could
have* touched *you*! *Happens*

time to time, I say, *you
down your pants in public*

& someone touches something.
You

look away. *You do this often,*
you say: *You're into anonymous*

sex. You say these last words
like I would say *nuclear waste*.

You do manage to come—
though you wouldn't trust

my major orifices, & would
have whipped out a wash &

dry for my hand if you
had one. & now it's time

for word games & goodbye:
I'm thinking of a phrase:

Whore without religion.
If you go looking

for romance on Anderson
Bridge, honey, you

just might find one.

Voyeur

Your window faces my window,
you have a bigger cock than mine,
it dangles as you go to bed. My

hunger is greater than yours.   I

watch you when I can, I watch
you when your lights are on,
when your shade's not drawn,

when you're alone,
alone.

How I'd love to walk
a plank, play pirate

with you. I'd lick
your dagger, your
wooden leg, the black
patch over your left
eye oh yes I'd call

you *Bluebeard*, you'd
not dangle on your way

to bed; I'd not pull down
the shade: someone

might need the view:
might still be me,

trapped on a burning ship,
looking to cross the way.

Instant

We meet in a hallway, halfway between Men's & Ladies'
at the South Station fuck film cinema on a
rainy Sunday, Mother's Day afternoon. None of this

crosses our minds at the time. We
make signals that work, we do not use words, &

after someone else
                          unzips your fly I'm
down on you.

The silent men
who have smoked, & stared, & stood along walls
until now
swoop in on us. Rough hands
push my head to your hair
three times: a voice
too near my ear
tells me: "SUCK IT, BABY!"
                          (We've been watching
Kansas City Trucking Company,
vocabularies & cocks have grown
with a fresh *bon mot* or two.)

                          Oh well
there's a mouth on each of your tits
but it's my mouth you come in, & you

leave, pants up quick but you kiss me,

& though other fingers probe me hungrily
—for I made suck sounds in this silence—
I leave too, & do not look for you.

Loveability Zero

We never need the same thing
in the same way
at the same time. If you turn

from me
when I touch your tit, your
glorious ass, hard cock

in the night & you're
love-dreaming
a different man, a
different touch, slap
my hand, shout my name
as you would *"Shit!",* it

is inevitable
that in things separate &
stormy as
people
    needs will be
varied, each & every touch,
hunger, request
not necessarily reciprocal.

I love you, Orolin John; it
is not games I play, or
merely horniness left-
over from empty-handed

returns from bars. It is more

than your skin I reach for,
more than your
body you must

deny me

On the Roof

Chutney's in heat   male dogs roam round
Chuck & Bob's house all night, silently,

sometimes biting each other, but with-
out sound, as if to avoid the catcher:

faggots cruising.   I too

am in heat, howl
in my boring human way, no man
in sight, in mind, for miles.

What if Bob & Chuck let Chutney loose?
What if we did not limit dog society?
What if one of us howled from a roof
until a person came?   In heat, in
uniform, *both*.

Cruising Athletes from a Sunny Window in Lamont

I

This is too far: this road, this
time, this trip to the bathroom.

Naked, writhing in a stall, alone!
Peep show for a masturbator, when

it's making love I need.   One
must delimit: decide how far

to go, & then
go there.   Or
not go there.   *But know.*

II

The macho future leaders of
American finance   & mores   are

still boys in sweatpants: wet,
unspankable: there

there   there
  there
    there: running:

102

each model on his college lawn,
I'll die without, within

this community of youth
& aloofness.   *He*

bends to throw a frisbee
to his buddy   both half
naked in this first warmth.

O to be flexible & personal
as their jock straps!   O

how acceptable proximity
might breed poems: *Poems*

of Consummated Love: The
Pulitzer, the Bollingen,

the National Book Award this year
go to a soiled athletic support.

III

Two firm butts   broader than the
   minds above

            not yet attached

or stretched to imagine

this lust going on
behind double glass
this unopenable window.

Shame

This was what separated
me from the sexual race:
He hesitated in Nini's Corner,

stared at the crosswords;
Hesitant: four feet away,
wanted;   eyed my eyes;

turned into the gay corner,
drew *Drummer*, idly,
nervously,   paged

They don't have my brand
of smoke   the counter man
told me, I

told myself they don't
have my brand of man, I
turned, I left the store!—

nothing to suck on, deserving
it, treating desire
like a dirty trick.

The Marks of Fairy Tales

In my version the prince
doesn't come thru thorns,

he comes on them, as he,
magician too, levitates

me: suspended over forest
by whimsical harness;

& I too come for thorns:
as they shred my kaftan

skin exposed & reddened
hurls toward you, *yours.*

But the prince is annoyed:
Your body's bruised, he

whines: *Will you look at
what you've done to those*

burns?   *Not 'til*

I've befriended a mirror,
milord,   & turning I add:

Every fairy princess is
entitled to his own tail.

The Poet Falls, Flags & Willowtrees

Laura Riding, exquisite poet, renounced
poetry. I am not surprised. Often I am

embarrassed, waving out here, a gaudy flag
from no known country,

tattooed & purple, always the foreigner
in a tightassed & tasteful New England town.

How few of us
walk naked, or in funny clothes;

alone: naked.   Alone: in funny clothes,
sitting up night long coughing lines out—

but these lungs never clear, the breaths,
though diseased, smoke-diminished,
non-commissioned, given no set direction

for an entrance, *keep coming*; I wave

like a willow, yellowed
somewhat weakened by

redundant inspirations: tremulous, neurotic,
ambitious, penis or pen ever in hand,
gesticulating to the populace,

always trying
to get it published.

Silk Scarves & Hard Leather

Silk scarves & hard leather, one for
expression, one for armor.

Black silk dresses, running shoes:
simplicity, necessity; two:

always two: one that orders,
one to spit-shine the shoe.

I wanted vagaries, naked dancing,
never needing more than the right dress

for the right emergency. I've got
plaid shirts, I've got blue jeans, I

leave my ear-rings home, send
safer clothes on errands.

Silk scarves tied into helmets,
hard leather high heel running shoes—

What floor are we dancing on? Whose are
these steps, from which direction

does music still dare to come,
in what costume?

Circles Might Lead to Rectangular Beds, Straight Lines Don't

O, yes—I too come here
merely to watch sculls
skim the river: Had I

told him *that*—not
I'm looking for a man,
& you're…

certainly a man.

THE SKY OVER CAMBRIDGE
is bluer than Oz! How
he'd have preferred that

to: *You look like a runner.*
But he did. & bolt he did,

he ran. Had I invited him
to play frisbee
we'd still be in bed.

Some of Us Wear Pink Triangles

for Rudy Kikel

At the Lesbian & Gay Pride March we
strode through main streets shouting
"Two/four/six/eight: Gay is just
as good as straight." Their hundreds
looked at our thousands. Some threw
insults, some supported. Most were
silent. We were noisy inside the
shelter of numbers. Balloons flew
into the face of the sky, forcing
all to see: *We are everywhere.*

At a dinner party in Somerville,
eight of us sit talking about music,
gay politics, gay literature, gay
love. In the conversation's first
lull we hear it: First come wolf
whistles, then: "Hey! Why don't
you guys look out? Lots of beautiful
guys on the sidewalk down here. You
talking about Anita Bryant up there?
You drinking any orange juice? Hey—
play us some more Beethoven." We

look at each other, trying to find
words. Rudy talks of gays beat up

after trying to throw a gay-straight
party. Kenny's been hit by a beer
bottle the night before. He'd had
his arm about a man. We all have
our stories. Then: THUD!—
Patrick hears it, I hear it, something's
been thrown against the house. Twice
more it happens, & laughter, & whistles,

& then: "Goodnight, guys. See ya
tomorrow." Already we've been moving
from windows & changing
the subject. But there's no room
for music now, & literature seems

removed. No matter how real Henry James
can make a character, *we* have to deal with
characters in the street, we have to
get from here to there & worry about
survival between Ball & Harvard squares.

Once Bruce told me he'd try gay sex, only
he'd never want to be branded *homosexual*.
I used to laugh.

Invisible History

My shrink told me it was unnatural to be
obsessed with the Nazi extermination of
homosexuals Look at me I'm normal he

said I sleep nights & I'm healthy enough
to listen to your stories & others worse than
yours & I still have sex & *I'm* Jewish so

what's with these nightmare pogroms   find
yourself a hot guy to go to bed with or
do it on the floor of his car but

stop it with these death camps. I
knew he was right, that his people had
lost millions more than my people, but

piles of emaciated   tortured   worked-to-
death   gassed-to-death   clubbed-to-death
bodies   resemble each other   & they

resemble *us* Look at that man on top
of the others Look at his beard He
could be me. When I was six my

father first told me about liberation
of the camps   by the Allies   he was
US Army & they entered at

last & those bodies, he said   those bodies.
By time I was 15 my eye doctor showed
mercy to me put me on sleeping pills

Circles around my eyes   I told him I
couldn't sleep & when I did fall I
found myself behind wire—barbed,

or electric: my head shaved   an empty
expression leering back at me   at every-
one in this odd century of horror

so systematic so organized. I'll give you
these pills he said   But don't abuse them
& cut out the fantasies, you're not even

Jewish

Neurotic Singlet

for B.D.

I'm too nervous to enjoy ya; *love just gives me paranoia.*

Still Life, with Dull Glow

Back here in stranger land—
my almost former lover's kitchen,
I make notes on the table, take
note of dull wood spoons, duller
pewter, dented. I still love him.
The rice is boiling, we've un-
corked a bottle of his favorite
non-Gallo wine, & it's breathing.
He's fussy that way, & I never
complain. "*Never complain*," my
mother told me, & maybe I'd
never be alone. She was alone,
but her words got me this far,
if this is measurable distance,
drying spoons, counting place
settings, & not complaining.

Finding Appropriate Gestures

for Pat Kuras

I wanted to sing a blues song.
They said: *White boys can't*

sing the blues. I wanted
to sing a torch song. They said:

Men don't do that. I wanted
to sing a showtune. They said:

You don't live on a stage. I

wanted to sing "Don Juan's
Reckless Daughter." They said:

You're nobody's daughter. I
wanted to sing

"Spring Can Really Hang You Up
the Most." They said:

It ain't even spring. So I sang
"It Might as Well Be Spring,"

a cappella, gave them all
the finger.

Whimsical Spring Poem (Harvard Man I)

Harvard man, Harvard man,
blond for no reason. I'd
sure as shit quit the Quad
for him, scratch every dance
from my card for him; kiss
sunshine goodbye to open
his fly; trade clothes
for sheets, miss other meets
for him, for him—

Lingering in a Silk Shirt

(1994)

Ragged Denim

Jude

Pull it this was love
Don't call it other names
This voice calling every
Eighteen months or so to
Fill the listener in on
What he's missed since

Departure Whatever it
Turned into while it was
Going on, when it stopped
It evolved into Love

Though you've both become
Too wise to try it again
[the physical part, the
Valentines & Crisco] the
Phone in your hand is his
Dick, the earpiece
Your ass, the voice still
His voice, yours, *yours*,
The wires, the love, pull
It, but not, this time,
Too hard

Propriety

George has a motorbike I won't go on it
not because George never had a car
license & this is a whole new thing but

in my youth Victor Clayman took me for
so many rides I bought my own crash
helmet & when we pulled into my father's

garage next to the Nova I'd pull Victor
down on the sawdust on the
motor oil suck his cock his big

handsome arms wrapped round my shoulders
my fingers sliding into his wide ass he
always came so much more slowly than he

drove even so we both kept
our helmets on

1969

In college Nana's sandwiches
were delivered until 3 a.m.

He'd arrive in a black Lincoln
Continental, open the trunk,

pull out enormous heroes
wrapped in waxed paper tucked

neatly into brown bags:
pounds of food, actually, and

$2.75? If it was
pre-midnight we'd

opt for a walk:
Main Street, Chez Joey's,

never tiring of Mafia
speculations, slice after

slice, or heroes
famed for sheer volume of

olive oil. It oozed from
tomato slices, onion and lettuce,

as we oozed excitement over

poems or prose just discovered

or that we would write

Fragrances and Carcinogens

The *Body Politic's* cartoonist Gary Ostrom wore
Fracas and smoked Rothmans when he made love
with Michael and me; for months I visited

department store cosmetic counters and airport
giftshops to find a bottle of that particular
cologne. The cigarettes were easier, packaged

in blue and white boxes, sold in complicated
general stores everywhere; luckily he had not
smoked King Sanos or Fatimas. For years smoke

and scent brought our ménage à trois back, as
Elizabeth Arden's Sandalwood recalled my un-
official high school breakdown, where in

emulation of my peer Jaqueline Neely I wore
the same outfit everyday, and listened over and
over to Barbra Streisand's first two albums, new

then, insisting later they alone had saved my
life. Was it Sandalwood or heartache that my
friend Alan would bring me out, teach me to

inhale and suck and then leave me, my nose in
my cologne bottle, not even his brand.

Sleep and Trust

John says he does not believe in rape. This poem
is not fucking him. John believes conquest is the

essence of heterosexuality, that no is not No,
there is a no that is less than No, when a woman

goes out drinking with four male college friends
she knows that if she loses consciousness she

will wake up raped, being raped, to be raped
again, only it is not rape, it is sloppy love-

making. Inebriation among the enemy is obviously
a resounding Yes, or perhaps a teasing Maybe. John

is a lawyer, he says the men should not be on trial
for rape, that it was understood by the woman, before

the drinks, before oblivion, that on some level, if
only the sexual, this is what she wanted, this is

what she expected.

9 October 1987

Art and Remembrance

They traumatized a Yugoslavian orphan
to make a U.S. tv miniseries. A
formidable actor held the 3-yr.-old

upside down off & on for several
hours while a woman playing
his or her mother screamed. She

has to blow the Nazi or see the
child put on the junk heap. Finally
someone in the silent mass of crew

people complains and the child is
released. An American actor child
is brought in, does the scene, and

gets to be in the final version.
Faced with a petition of names of
crew members who had witnessed the

all-for-art debacle, the producers
said, "We thought it was a good
opportunity for an orphan to make

some money." But—what is the figure
on the check? Will it be enough to pay
for the child's first therapy session?

29 April 1989

For Carl Wittman

Everywhere along the route he
was magnanimous Dance
notation Celebration Long
hair short Hair never
fashionable, & moles. Warts
& all met college kids
Lamont questions: What were
the 60s like? He
wasn't impressed Bob
Moses lives in Cambridge-
port, passed the house
each day. He'd rather
argue Bach more emotional
than Mozart, or why
Praetorious dances & rock
don't. Incurable dishwasher
I'm rinsing He comes
up behind, hugs, says:
Don't you ever want
to break them all? Meaning?
Enamored with the
written word but no
correspondent he'd in-
frequently thank for
altered drafts poems
to Durham but he'd prefer
being stranger in Yugoslavia
desex-roling ancient
Dances.

Cornwall's Servant

He's a stupid old man, dividing
his kingdom during his life,
his weak old age, and giving
the pieces to two such wicked
daughters merely because they
could verbalize his vanities.
Surely he must have known what
evil hearts they bore; or perhaps
he'd spent no quality time in
their company. Maybe he re-
membered little girls with ribbons
and dolls. But shit hit the fan,
the kingdom crumbled, I could not
stand there and watch my lord
blinded and maimed, and do nothing.
I took my stand, I entered the
manic action, I fought back, I
was slain—and for that, or
despite it my character's provided
with no name. I am known, by
those who read the story at all,
by my position, and by my lord.

There are no snapshots of my mother. —Maxine Hong Kingston, *The Woman Warrior*

My mother doesn't *do* snapshots—there has to be
a pose, stiff-smiled, as much a mask

in 1939 as in 1990. Once my camera

caught her squinting in the glare
of the sun on the Great South Bay

and she never forgave me. "How could you do
that?" she demanded, "Tear up that awful

picture." Instead I bought
a plastic frame, hung it on a nail

on my Harvard office wall, so that anyone
curious in academia could see

where I'm from. My father, at her side,
stares openly into the camera, pleased

with his new hat, seemingly
oblivious of the basiloma

craters on his nose

Eminent Domain

The house I grew up in
is being torn down
The modest five room bungalow
behind a Cities Service gas station
was too close to the intersection
of Route 112 and Sunrise Highway
The State of New York won't allow
my folks, in their late 70s, to
die there. The house I grew up in
is going to be the flat center of
a cloverleaf bypass.

The house I grew up in was built
in 1950 by John Sequino. It had
two bedrooms, a living room, a
kitchen not large enough to eat in
& a front porch. We used to play
Monopoly behind the screens, drinking
Kool Aid out of vividly colored
aluminum tumblers. We called them
aluminum *glasses*. My mother saves
nothing, I can't show you one.

The house I grew up in was hardly
singular, there were four of them
on a six-house dead-end block. We
relinquished our front porch in 1960,
when my parents hired two German

college students to build a room on
the porch's foundation. For years
this room would be the center of family
life for the three of us, but recently
it was too close to the street for my
mother, & it dwindled to a mud room.

How many secrets are in the house I
grew up in? I know where
my cat Dolly's buried. I know that
behind the radiator in my bedroom my
Lone Ranger-Tonto wallpaper still
exists, there was never a brush so
narrow, and my father always boasted
he painted the whole interior in a day.
I know the places he missed, where last
year's peach is not this year's peach.

The biggest & best secret of the house
I grew up in is not my secret but my
father's, which is as it should be. Down
in the basement's southeast corner was
his workroom, every 50s husband wanted or
had one, & its focal point was a mammoth
work table: iron pipes across which lay
a huge thick dense plank of wood. On my
last visit to the house I grew up in I
went down to the basement. My father had
hacked his table to jagged pieces. No one
would ever use this table, no one strong
enough to carry it away the way he carried

it here, no one would ever carry it away.

My father made sure he had one hand in the
destruction of his home. My father, returned
from WWII to the American suburbs, grateful,
hopeful, ready to settle in

24 April 1989

Rationale

When we "love" we are looking for
the perfection designed to turn

our friends envy-green, and a hand
that, extended, is there to

extract us from the mire. When we "love"
we seek the joyous expressions of

tv commercials, the two-story houses
of favorite sitcoms, the other half

one hears so much about. *I gave up
smoking for my other half. My better*

half's home with the flu. When we "love"
we are insuring against

dateless movies, diminishing chances
to take autumnal foliage drives

outside the city. When we "love" we
sometimes consider our final moments:

will they be witnessed? Dying alone,
living alone, all too horrible—

He was found weeks later, the mail carrier

noticed a smell. Just his luck to die

in February, they had to wait for the thaw.
When in "love" we peruse Valentines and

perforated perfume ads in magazines, we
wish to be more attractive than usual

because now we have half of a couple's image
to uphold: are we social enough, can we throw

a good party? How many Christmas cards
grace our wall? Did everyone remember to

write both our names on the outside envelope?

Choice

I'd rather be pregnant with life
I did not cherish or want than be
carrying HIV in my veins but that's

not my choice. Were I pregnant maybe
I'd bring forth life in gratitude but
in case that were not the case I'd

want the right to consider the life
not nonlife but not a life true and
separate as my own, a part of my

biology that, like cancer, might be
blessedly removed from me, allowing
me to continue solitary, and myself

Serious Irises

To witness the truly serious irises
one must pilgrimage to the corner

of Linnaean Street and Avon Hill,
where a wood two-story is bordered

on two sides by a meticulously
planted garden which in May boasts

at least a dozen varieties of very
large irises, blueblack and copper

beards, the palest of yellows, tied
up with sticks to support the weight

of the big blooms. This is that
garden's spectacular moment, just as

the garden at Swedenborg Chapel is
an early spring garden, filled with

croci, daffodils, hyacinths, tulips
including little snarling parrots;

now it's mid-July and the ornamental
onions push puce pompoms into the

clear hot Cantabrigian air, no
doubt celebrating Bastille Day.

Arnold

for Alison

If we live long enough we
outlive too many, & without

the familiar our lives seem
fragile, Steuben glass

figures we cannot afford, each
gift has its pricetag.

In Style Again

Armed with a classic shirt
from a previous era,

memorized lyrics to hundreds
of American songs, and enough

gray hair to inspire anyone
to call me Daddy I

go to the gym, HIV
positive, rubbers in

my knapsack, ready
for anything, even

explanations.

The Luck of the Draw

Sometimes gloom itself
acts as a muse. It

begins as a bad mood,
then expands to

a meditative misery
from which poetic

thought proceeds. It
could also lead to suicide.

This is the barbed wire
fence some of us straddle:

our eyes seeking star
constellations, our

crotches bloodied;
our inner selves

mutilated, awaiting
miracles: his call.

Calendar

Acupuncture this afternoon
Pentamidine tomorrow

Nurses suggest vacation
hejira from boredom & fear

: but really—travelling
with all those pills!

Infection suggests stasis.
Death is a resort we

could visit; could afford:
if not the kindness of

Seconals, Jerzy Kosinski's plastic
bag, recommended by the Hemlock

Society. It is late spring,
lush spring, the peonies,

roses, irises have followed
the tulips, magnolia, and

dogwood, which
followed the daffodils,

narcissus, and jonquils,
which followed the croci,

which followed the croci.

Driving the Stake Through My Father's Heart

Had he been the type of vampire I could enjoy
—avuncular, vital, a passion for his work—

death—life—maybe I could have loved him
and not gone through such hoopla to exorcise

paternity. After all, it wasn't easy: constantly
hoping he'd forget the sunrise, or we'd

meet in the kitchen by the garlic cloves,
or I'd find the Crucifix Grandma left behind—

maternal Grandma—I had to sharpen the stake,
and being a clumsy sort, often cut myself—

look at my knuckles—you assumed I was recycling
cat food cans—sharp edges are interchangeable,

and certain lives not mutually supportable. He
couldn't appreciate my life choices or my poetry,

I had to drive it through his heart

Visitation & Mortality

We are mysteries to each other, the butcher, the seamstress, the poet, though we shared for 19 years a bungalow 'til you sent me from my 50s childhood to my late 60s campus adolescence. You were brave, I never returned. Now, aged 40, on thrice annual visits "home" you ask me: "Would you move back?" "No!" I snap, too definitely.

Later, in a department store my mother faints in my arms, as I ease her fragile body to the linoleum floor I wonder, Is this…dead away? I yell for help, a man folds his hooded sweatshirt, navy blue, *Here, put this under her head.* A woman with a small child, a son, introduces herself: *I'm a nurse, can I be of help?* Yes, I say, please, she drops to her knees beside me, takes my mother's pulse. It's there. Police arrive, male, female, tell me an ambulance has been summoned. *I don't want an ambulance!* says my mother, quietly, firmly, reappearing behind glazed eyes. I don't want an ambulance. We struggle to keep her on the floor a bit longer, then with all hands on her she is back on her feet. The policewoman drives us home. My mother's appalled, what will the neighbors she thinks nothing of, think of her?

We reenter the five rooms I grew up in, the home of her high energized 30s and 40s and 50s. *I don't want Daddy to know,* she says as she changes her clothes. *He'll tell everyone.* I say nothing, I am not supposed to say anything here, we both know it will become one of our secrets, like snuck luncheons at Bronco Charlie's, J&B Scotch beneath the kitchen sink, sloe gin in my bedroom closet, my gayness. That night she prepares dinner, two days later she insists on taking me by taxi to my train. Standing alone at trackside, knocking yellowjackets out of her way with her large beige leather handbag, her cheap watch dangling by the stainless steel whistle she incessantly carries in case something scary happens to her.

Twins

Two. Of course there are
two: identical twins. My

maternal grandmother bore
three sets: boys, boy/girl,

girls, of whom my mother is
one. The flu epidemic of

1918 took the boys, the girls
are near 80. *Girls* is what

my mother calls them, her-
self, all women. When I

was a girl I marveled at
their energy, mother's, aunt's,

that volume doubled. "Walt,
that shirt is be-u-tee-full,"

—in stereo. My mother's four
operations, gradual hysterectomy,

expensive aftermath of her
difficult childbirth—mine—

—hers—Aunt Ali trying to

fool me, meeting me at

elementary school, making lunch
in my mother's floral apron.

Widowed, my aunt moved to
Florida. Now Lena and Lichi

live in Venice; Netha, my
mother, Edna to all others,

has not seen Alice 15 years.
I flew to Sarasota to fill

gaps. Alice wore her cheeriest
clothes for me, showed me her

hibiscus, whispered how she
missed Harry—the only muted

words her Lithium and her and
Netha's energy levels allow.

The twins have always confused
volume with merriment. Maybe

it was difficult otherwise being
heard, being one voice; perhaps

it was the attempt at communication
over the din in a room filled with

treadle sewing machines operated by
so many girls, including those

Libi Twins, who left school at 14
for "the sweat shop." Maybe that's

when and where they started yelling.

Nylon Lycra

New Brunswick

Billie Holiday had recently returned
from being the toast of Europe, and was

walking down a Harlem street after
being in a midtown café brawl. Shaken by

racial epithets hurled, she later ran
into a friend who asked, "Billie, how

are you?" "Well, you know," said Lady
Day, "I'm still a n----- here." After

the first night of the fifth annual
Lesbian & Gay Studies Conference Michael

& I were walking to our hotel on George
Street when two Aryan lads in a Toyota

pick-up circled and yelled HEY FAGGOTS!
It wasn't until I was brushing my teeth,

had showered & put on the conference tee
shirt that the energy of our tribe came

back to me, I laughed as I spit: I am
a faggot everywhere, but especially in

New Brunswick.

Frank O'Hara Homage at Harvard

If you are dead long enough
And famous hard enough people

Devise ways to strip you,
Replace you with

Charming anecdotes If you
Sucked cock you'll be

Single and eccentric,
A lover of architecture

And good food. If you
Roamed the spray halls

At the Indoor Athletic Building
Scanning clandestine hard-ons

They'll have you adoring the hawthorns
Lining Mem Drive, not mentioning

It's the way to the Bird Sanctuary.
Soon you'll have died someplace

Less compromising than Fire Island,
And lush lyrics about Lana, Liz

And Marilyn will be used to

Prove your heterosexuality,

Buried, to be sure, in East Hampton

Artistry & Hypochondria

Because the early death of William Kapell
proved to you travelling pianists were
the endangered species you envisioned

yourself *Yourself* to be, you decided
to no longer fly Plunging your hands
and forearms into scalding water before

concerts was not enough Sweaters & scarves
and long winter coats all year around not
enough Portable heaters placed around your

instrument in a recital hall in Jerusalem
not enough Mrs. Bernstein bending you over
a sink to wash and cut your neglected hair,

not enough, visiting Eugene Ormandy's favorite
orthopedist in Philadelphia, not enough,
chronic colds and influenza, not enough, your

travelling case boasting three tiers of
prescription drugs, uppers and downers,
Luminal, Nembutal, *not enough,* O Glenn Gould

had you only survived to the age of AIDS

For Mitzel

Hello. I'm Gogi Grant, and I have AIDS. I had a hit record in 1956, "The Wayward Wind." Some folks wonder why I've gone public with my AIDS, they also say "Why *you*, Gogi?" I nod my head, why me indeed, I say, I know I have this perfectly good husband, but there have always been truck drivers. I always loved diners and truck stops. I remember this man coming up to me at a silver special, taking off his hat and saying, Miss Grant, my wife and I have worn another hole in our third copy of "The Wayward Wind." I blushed and said, What do you do with it?

My husband said the other day, Well Gogi, I hope you don't get this CMV retinitis, because I'd hate to see you lose your eyesight. There are so few, so few left who can distinguish 19 shades of chartreuse.

Well, I said, just the other day little Henry Matrice came down the street and said to me, Mrs. Grant, you're looking absolutely puce today. So, in the midst of adversity, there is hope. Hope and AZT.

My husband said to me, well, Gogi, I fear a lot of things, but I have this feeling if you get the AIDS dementia, neither of us will ever know it.

This was my hit song:

> *O I met him down*
> *in a railroad town*
> *back in the younger day*
> *And the lonesome sound*
> *of the outward bound*

Made him a slave
to the wandering way
O the wayward wind

For Tipper Gore

Those who'd like the right to say *you can't*
To Prince, AC/DC, & Adam Ant—
I hasten to alert you to the danger
Of lyrics, situations, even stranger.

Why not apply your censorious rage
To the truly lurid…opera stage?

Consider the Princess Salomé,
Having failed getting John the Baptist to lay
With her sheds veils for the Christian's head
Dances for Step Dad, Herod,
Who orders soldiers to squash her dead

: *die Liebe bitter schmecke* * indeed,
Opera warnings are what kids need.

Pre-Nazi Strauss was merely a bother,
But Manon Lescaut LOVED her brother;
Thais dances minus tutu,
A lesbian admires Lulu.

If blood & guts tend to upset you
Sticker-up your *Rigoletto*.
There's torture in *Tosca* & *Turandot*,
& Carmen's tied up by Don Jose's knot.

The grander the opera, the more potent

The taints—
The only thing kinkier
I~ *Li~~ ~f ~h~ S~~~~*

*"the bitter taste of love": Hedwig Lachmann's libretto for Richard Strauss's 1905 opera was a German translation and abridgement of Oscar Wilde's *Salomé*.

Legend Has It

When Jack Paar asked Judy Garland how it felt
to be a legend, she

cleared her throat, and said hoarsely,
"It's peculiar." A consummate singer,

she knew the weight of the word, the
designation of intonation. Sometimes a drunken

slur, a drugged pause, an awkward
silence   two beats too long

denote damaged brilliance, the luck of the fall,
of the falling

      "It's peculiar," she said,

"They think—'O—we can't call her—
she's a legend—'

"And I sit by the phone Saturday nights
waiting for it to ring."

Watching Sting on *Saturday Night Live*

Sting is wearing this long black coat
& low cut shirt when he stops
singing another soloist plays &

Sting sits in a chair looking
down like he'd hit a wrong
note & felt shame. His

pants are very baggy maybe
his shirt's a leotard top
When Mick holds his mike

you think, he's holding my
cock, & now he's gonna
suck it With Sting you feel

you both got out of this space
vehicle, couldn't hear your
mother's voice calling

Dinner! but instead just
walked the banks of a
river, not knowing if its water

was poison; was pure

While Looking at a Photograph of Barbra Streisand in *Life* Magazine

White lady in your white living room
The deep fire glittering inside your
thrift shop dresses is gone, gone

with the awkwardness of youth &
legendary repertoire. There won't be
obscure ditties sung in odd tempos,

but meticulously laid-out rooms, in-
numberable houses, possessions in-
cluding The Gift, surfacing now

in a set of polished performances,
the artistry of composing a room,
monotone, magistral, imposing in

its lack of vibrant surfaces. No red,
but soft green glows outside your
classic windows, gorgeous & un-

expected, white jade's glow when
held by an entrance to twilight. That you,
raised in a tenement on the other ocean,

the other side of vicious chance, could
bring together all these shades of
whiteness, pristine, unpenetrable (guarded

not only by dogs & guns, but learned taste),
your arms outstretched, *Mine!*, this world,
you say, right, of course, controlled,

perhaps cold, but unceasingly resonant as
your voice, the vehicle of your fantasy
destiny

Vision of Love

Before Mariah Carey was born
I entertained a Vision of

Love; like my mother her
Blue Moon, her Blue Heaven,

I'd conjured the occasional
handsome man who'd be my

friend, and love me harder than
diamonds. My Vision of Love

never became a hit single, and
did not coincide with real

tangible, viable, love, longevity
for which Michael and I struggled

against societal nonconcern, the
virus decimating our generation,

and doing it without topping the
charts. And yet, were it not for

the silver bullet hits that made life
choreographable, how dull it might

have been, how danceless

Sooner or Later

In a white Bob Mackie gown and wrap
from which ermine gewgads dangle

Madonna shimmies and purrs through her
personalized Sondheim lyrics, says she

always gets her man. Maybe she does,
and maybe Sondheim does too. But those

of us who've learned the lash of the whip
of rejection know the value of a good

black dress, eyes that look a bit vague
or even frightened, finding a spot of

—could it be hope?—in the distance,
and singing the lyric without embellish-

ments. Our bowels long ago reached melt-
down, the cold douche of sooner or later

finding nothing purified us, simplified
our wardrobes, chastened our delivery

For John Wieners

In Provincetown 1991
the drag queen starring
in two Charles Busch plays

has very muscular arms.

Since the one Busch play
incorporates a line from
The Boys in the Band I shall
quote another: "I hurt my heels
doing chin-ups."—"You shouldn't
do chin-ups in heels."

Drag queens, flowers, and women
who sing are still the fulcrum
of my teeter-totter.

New Paltz 1991

This is the river Native American
legend says if you were happy
here you return to die. The crickets,

the soft red moon, do set eternity
a place at the summer table: a bearded
man sitting on the cemetery wall could

be candidate for a final fling. Two women
walk their dogs; my friends and I walk
Huguenot Street talking softly. The false

French windows of my first apartment are
dark as they are unopenable, expensive
garbage (a yacht, an outboard motor,

barbecue equipment) now mar the view
of sunsets over Mount Mohonk, beyond the
north-flowing Wallkill River, over the

flats from which comes our excellent corn,
the current flavor that transcends memory.

The J. Poems

Things I Cannot Bring You

An unsullied past—not that I'd
want to; an uninfected bloodstream
—would that I could—a person

scraped of memories—No, simply
scarred & frightened, a spirit
that wavers, a mouth fearful

of deep kisses, a list of
don't-do's at the ready but also
me, do-do-do, at the ready

1 January 91

I Know Your Name

I see you on your bicycle, it's

a night too cold to ride, I'm
walking briskly with my

train-bound lover I don't
shout your name you turn

into our street you know
where I live Do you

want to see me or
are you picking up

take-home at Cremaldi's?
How do I muster

romance in the face of
HIV infection, daily

terrors & uncertainties,
after several years of

moving in a haze and getting
silly over no one? And what do

you want? You're rather a mystery,
you appear not really happy but

complete in yourself, you smile
at me but no more than you

smile walking or riding by yourself
I've told you more about me than you

have about you, this only feeds my
hyperactive imagination

What are you thinking?
What are you needing?

You coolly say when you've
finished your local studies

you'll move to
New York or L.A.

New York or LA.!
I've not experienced

the interior of your
mind or even your
apartment We've
shaken hands, what we

take away from these
encounters is, I

suppose, our individual
businesses, take-outs,

nourishments we
separately fancy

Tribute

Flowers you bring me have too
much significance surely you

didn't intend the heather to
root in my heart. Why did

white tulips last two weeks
in aseasonally warm weather?

—Just because I cut their
stem bottoms biweekly, kept

their water clean, lukewarm?

19 February 91

Dishes

Michael left the dinner table
to drive to the airport, his
brother was back from St. Croix.

I looked at you across the
empty dishes & said, I have the
AIDS virus, *I'll never*

open my mouth flowerlike for
rain to enter another. You had
already made your decision, & I

had clearing to do.

20 February-21 March 91

7 Embarrassments in the Wrong Key

1. Impeccable, not Peckable

Catholic University or
repressive parents taught you
posture you can't forget You

don't easily sit or
squat or lay down. Free
weights & Nautilus have

defined rigidity. True,
you are something to behold,
as fine-featured & polite

as any of my acquaintance.
Maybe you'd say Thank You
for a blow job, it's

happened before. Were I
the trigger of your desire
I'd still need the stamina

to unravel the knots
of your good manners

2.

Amtrak ticket holders

are folders depicting a

toothbrush captioned *Have
you forgotten anything else?*

I remember my name, my address,
my telephone number, the way your

figure gets smaller & your black &
white check trousers turn soft gray

as you retreat. Your wardrobe was
chosen to assist your disappearance

but your eyes & smile belie
understatement of Ralph Lauren

You might as well be wearing
a red silk dress
I cannot forget you

3. Chant

There is no limit
to unrequited love

4. Postcard

Three crows on a winter-
naked tree, Keely Smith
singing Cole Porter's

"I'm in Love Again"

5. Abyss

Sometimes the gap
between who you are

& what I need & made
of you is so wide

so deep I drown

6. Remind Me

The image of beloved:
the serious man in beige
trousers standing on the
pedals of his bicycle
hatless on a cold night.
Only a romantic could
be him. Only a romantic
could see him.

7. Travel Journal

I was able to follow
all the directions, though they
changed thrice daily & the goal
& the players, too

I was able to find the local

soft rock station to ensure
mushy songs that would
make me think of you

Emotions sprawled
slatternlike on a soft
tired mattress once
the stage of my teenage ecstasy

Outlaws of Love

I used to think the woman who
repeatedly broke into David
Letterman's home claiming to be

his wife was odd. Now I pretend
you impregnate me before you
leave Cambridge.

21 February 91

Simple Gifts

Many years ago at the Club Baths
in Manhattan I met a dark youth
after hours of lovemaking. He too

was sated before he met me, and we
asked an attendant for a blanket,
it was coarse and gray, and this

young man and I lay on a dormitory
bleacher, with a mirror on the
bottom of the upper tier, four

feet above our heads. As we drifted
off I looked at our reflection and
I knew, this is all that I need.

On Thursday night you returned the
phone message I had left on your
machine, & I glowed for hours.

21 February 91

On Your Guard

The first time you came to see
me at home the Christmas tree

was up, it gave me the will
to insist you not leave until

you had climbed the stairs;
Ginger Rogers and Fred Astaire

glided through my mind:
your secrets I'd find

before the season was over
—I didn't blow your cover—

You were off on a skiing vacation
only I had the motivation

and nothing occurred,
though I grinned and purred

invited you across the moat
suggested you remove your coat

but you didn't desire
I couldn't aspire

to make your cock sing

You now study boxing

instead of romance
your opponent's no chance

to floor this golden boy.
I can still see your leap of joy

after your curtain call as Pangloss
in *Candide*, you've no albatross

but you still go to mass
with your marvelous ass

I confess need to steal
a glance as you kneel

27 February 91

Therapy

Unravel the obsession.
Begin here: he never
encouraged me. When I
feel pain he has not
called, when I feel
jealousy toward men he
may have slept with, may
be having sex with, this
has nothing to do with
him, he's never opened
that part of himself to
me. The man probably
knows nothing beyond I
am infatuated, write notes,
leave messages, get a silly
smile whenever I see him,
and suffer varying energy
levels

18 February 91

Wardrobe

I choose my clothes carefully
in case I run into you I wear

gray, I like gray but I wear it
so often now because you so

underdress, and a lot of your
muted earthtones are beige or

gray. Of course the one time
you praised something I wore it

was an agate and crystal ear-
ring hanging to my shoulder,

and you've touched me through
silk shirts twice, once aubergine,

once slate blue. When one cannot
be naked with someone it is good

to be appropriately clothed.

Incorrigible

The last thing I did the 11°
night I thought I'd be

joining you at the Brattle
to sit three hours at your

side watching Fellini's
La Dolce Vita was take two

condoms and two packets of
portable lube from my

dish on the dressing table.
Incorrigible is *the* word.

20 February 91

8:30 a.m.

Walking past your house
while your shades are

drawn I assume you are
asleep I tap the seat of

your bicycle locked today
to the street sign at the

corner instead of in its
alcove under the fire

escape I think about being
inside you & your apartment

it's time to go to work
I've never been invited

27 February 91

Last Year

I remember when it first snowed
in winter 1990-91, it started

almost midnight, I dressed for
a storm and entered one. Others

had preceded me, it is a college
town filled with the young,

skidding and making snowballs,
I cannot say there was that near-

silence of rural snow. I only
had two city blocks to go, one

to Mass Ave., one to Remington
and there like the setting of a

Henry James story stood the
rounded corners of Ware Hall,

the mammoth apartment building
that for two years housed you.

The story ends there. You were
not outside, romping in the snow,

I did not ring your buzzer, you

did not come to the door in

some garment you sleep in, there
was no shared hot cocoa or two

brandy snifters or the suggestion
I remove wet things. In my head

this scene would be replayed many
times, with alternate middles and

endings, only my walk into the
midnight snow actuality, but

all the variations honest, based
in desire, told in the right spirit.

17 December 91

Muscle Psyche

Maybe it's that you are still
in complete control of your
body; I watch you sometimes

from the pedestrian side of
the free weights room, you
so intense about your exercise

it becomes meditation: you, the
weights, the motion and the
mirror. And look what it's done:

you must, by now, be the image
you wanted, the man of your dreams
in the way in which you are the

man of mine. Times you've
instigated hugs your back seems
a barrier warriors require

7-20 March 91

In the Order

Sometimes when I'm feeling
crazy I pretend we're
monks, singing

Gregorian Chant like Enigma
& staring into each other's
eyes so intensely we

almost miss Vespers but you've
got this discipline & we
two-step in on time.

I would hate for your body
always to be obscured by
a robe, I'd miss your hooded

hair, but maybe our monastery
would have a swimming hole

28 February 91

Sanctus

I thought I would not be
in a state of grace I went

to the Paradise to look for
you, drank club soda alone

Talked to someone Positive
but he cringed at the mention

of my shingles. I thought I
would not be in a state of
grace I went to Catholic mass

My doctor took communion I
bought bagels after the service
and as I drove home on my bike

my pocket bulging and fragrant
another bicyclist called out
my name. I stopped. I was

apparently in a state of
grace. It was you.

3 March 91

Worship

At Saint Paul's that Sunday
they did the *I am a jealous God,*
put no gods before me ultimatum.
I sat there in increasing
alienation, thinking, I am in
this church because of the
possibility of running into You.

12 March 91

Figurant

It's almost as if I expected
someone else to make the remainder

of my life extraordinary. Take my hand,
marvelous creature, lead me to

the rest of my life. An actor lover
would have been so apropos to the

terminally ill: the roles one could
play before oblivion took stage center, but

would pain not be pain despite persona?
No matter—it is not how the actor cast

himself, and the dramatis personae
of my dwindle returned to normal:

no last minute stars; all creative
temperament—mine

7 March 91

After Reading an Alfred Chester Story

Here it is Springtime & you not needing to take one walk with me the
nights not balmy but pleasant & I with this clay-colored sweat shirt,
taupe almost, no color at all but that of the earth & not even normal
earth, & you never calling or dropping by unexpectedly, me never
running accidentally into you. Today at the computer at work, tired &
worn out an instrument of another's words I suddenly looked at the open
door & thought You could find out where my office is & come by as a
surprise. Isn't it odd how even anger & a too intimate familiarity with
neglect never totally do in hope? I wear the gray shirt with a colorful
tee underneath, thinking daily, well, maybe, all the tirades my heart
choreographs against you make me mad but never do I stop thinking
oh, maybe, not even now that it is spring & if you had any viable juices
they'd flow & the knowledge I was so constantly available might mean
something on the night of a day made you too tired to roam for someone
who'd look to you like you look to me

23-24 April 91

Never Ever

Never wanted to own you
Never wanted to keep
you naked in a small
space Never wanted to
straddle your chest and
shit on your pectorals,
never wanted to piss on
your face. Never wanted
to shave your pubes, tattoo
my initials in their absence.

Never wanted to see your
wardrobe diminished to a dog
collar, never cared to hear
your already limited vocabulary
reduced to *Woof! Woof!*
Never wanted to stand coolly
detached while my mean dyke
friend pierced your nipples,
never wanted to tug on the
subsequent chain.

Never wanted to take you to
Kenmore Square in your thong
and a raincoat, and leave
you there, in the rain. Never
wanted to supplant your God,
never wanted to take you to

Paradise on a leash, pop
Ecstasy in your mouth,
put you on all fours, have
you hum "I Could Have Danced
All Night," my fist filling
your excellent mouth. Never.

6 June 91

Occluded Front

Though I've never had you
I've become a master of giving

you up. The first time I saw
you I wanted you to have sex

with me. I wasn't expecting
miracles, I didn't assume

you'd reverse my AZT impotence,
I merely saw my brother in you,

and anticipated a great intimacy.
I did what I had to do to meet you,

discovered you had this hectic
schedule, I could not see you except

when I managed to meet you at our
mutual gym, or chance encounters in

our shared neighborhood; even there
I had to guard the distance between

us from me so as not to frighten
you with my intensity, my obvious

desire. I danced in place for you,

allowing my gestures and words to

express fondness, but with great
respect for your detachment. I feared

losing you altogether, you're transient
in the community of my living and

dying, but oh in my head we live in a
rural haven where time is immaterial,

my inappropriate infatuation, your
lack of it matters

little. We're both gentlemen, we
periodically lock eyes, sharing what

cannot be scheduled or misinterpreted.
We've never fucked, but the print of

you's tattooed on my soul, someday
you'll be in the shower or alone or

with someone else on your bed, you'll
notice odd markings on the insides of

your eye-lids the private places no one
goes, you'll see me

8-9 March 91

Riverside Cambridgeport, Winter

Two women with
children are feeding
the ducks. They waddle
out from under the
footbridge for bread
crumbs. Some hungers
are satiable; the thought
softens the ice they
slip on

A motor boat churns
through the icy Charles
in the hopeful thrust
I would bring towards

  you

19 February 91

Reality Check

Don't memorize
what he wore during
chance encounters You'll

always conjure his image
in flesh tones—the brown

eyes that seemed happy to
see you—the summer glow

on skin stretched over
those muscles; his clothes

so tight, so often black
or white, sometimes blue,

the blue you favor, and
favors you. How frequently

you've worn the same
combinations—as if you'd

dressed together. Other
than that you were rarely on

the same, as some call it
wavelength. You wanted, he

didn't. Now he's moving to
New York—he giggles, he'll

rent in Spanish Harlem. You
don't know when you'll have

energy for Amtrak. You know
he wouldn't meet your train.

12-13 August 91

Fin

There is a little U-Haul
doubleparked outside Ware
Hall, Harvard Street

entrance. Who is moving
out? Who is moving
in?

30 August 91

Blue Rayon

Diagnosis

When the doctor and the tests
confirm you are ill begin

to learn to breathe. Hold on to
a crystal your lover or your

god. Watch your favorite
tv shows read books

that teach or make you laugh
escape or go deeper Don't

smoke cigarettes or drink
alcohol; Take vitamins, eat

good food, keep working and
exercise Don't curse fate or

spend energy wishing things
were otherwise They're not

Today is still yours
Be good to it

31 October 1989

Breakfast in the 1990s

Each & every day is a
gift, waking up &

peeing & feeding the cat
looking in the mirror

Are there marks? How
unblurred the eyes? You

still look great, everyone
says. Take your

experimental drug, the brown
bottle left on the kitchen

table overnight, do six
salutes to the sun, the

tedious but essential back
exercises: pelvic tilt,

William's pose, the cat, three
circles with your knees cupped

in your hands, three
in each direction, grateful

for the feeling, for the

mobility. The drug absorbed

you sit across the table from
your lover, the old cat

between you on her own chair,
perhaps wondering what happened to

bacon breakfasts. Dry cereal
now, yogurt, skimmed milk,

seasonal berries

31 October 1989

The Mouth Poem

What if your mouth
were suddenly considered
a lethal weapon,

your saliva
could kill. How many deep

kisses would be yours?
Not having the freedom

to deposit semen freely
is no cage at all compared

to *that*: the shutting of the
mouth as a major entrance

into the body
into the soul
into the self

Away

I've HIV.
To avoid PCP
I inhaled monthly

AP, until in
collusion with ddI
it inflamed my

pancreas, elevated
my amylase. Now

I begin each day with
four 25 mg. Dapsone &

homemade AL-721, hopeful
membrane fluidizer.

On Phil Donahue on
March 1, 1990 several

people, mostly white
women under 45, said

gay men have to be put
away—in a desert, behind

fences; they said they could
not possibly raise children

with our images, with us,
around. Phil said, "You

mean, round them up like we
did the Japanese Americans

during World War II, or the
Jews during the holocaust."

"I don't care," said the woman
with the silver hoop earrings

the peasant blouse and the pony-
tail, "I just want them away.'

I've got 37 T-4 cells, dear;
patience.

2 March 1990

Transition in *Newsweek*

"If you die famous, or marry someone famous, or are born to famous parents, you might wind up in the Transition column in *Newsweek* magazine."

Mel Gibson died today after battling his third bout of PCP

Sylvester Stallone succumbed to pancreatitis due to the experimental drug ddI

Work on Eddie Murphy's newest film came to a halt when it was discovered amoebas were eating his corneas

Arnold Schwarzenegger's struggle with wasting syndrome has left the Republican at 80 pounds despite his $500 a day nourishment treatment

Tom Cruise has been unable to eat solid food for four months because of a pesky candida of the throat

Larry Bird's neuropathy has ended every sports lover's delight at seeing such a tall white man run around in little shorts

Tom Selleck's toxoplasmosis and lymphoma have made insurance on his new film with Goldie Hawn unlikely, although Ms. Hawn in a rare interview said that after seeing Kurt Russell tied to his bed in a diaper she can handle anything

Matthew Modine's short struggle against progressive multifocal

leukoencephalopathy ended today. Fortunately he was blind
and demented and did not know he wouldn't live to skip rope
in a jock strap in *Vision Quest II*, which now goes to Matt
Dillon if the CD4 trial keeps him fit

Mr. Rogers has killed himself after severe frustration at being unable to
figure out what plastic discs had to do with the slit holes on
his cardigan sweater

Pee Wee Herman died today of toxic shock after flying to China on
his special bike to try the cucumber. Before leaving the
Playhouse he told the kids his AZT would keep him safe
until the cure. **CURE!!** shouted the flowers and Globey
the talking globe. **CURE!!** shouted Chairry the chair, who
would miss Pee Wee's little butt. **CURE!!** shouted Jambi the
Genie, whose dementia had made him lose touch with his
powers. **CURE!!** shouted Mrs. Rene, who was tired of having
no gay male friends and never even got out of her quilted
housecoat anymore. **CURE!!** shouted the King of Cartoons
and absolutely everyone but Cowboy Curtis, dead of massive
internal KS. **CURE!!** was the secret word that day

23-24 May 1990

Empowerment

So it's a three-speed bike, built
between Korea & Vietnam, & somebody

else's (my lover's), & the first gear
skips, like the heart's beats,

but it enables me to fly over previously
unfamiliar terrain in my

chosen hometown. My headband is
my helmet, my baggy corduroys

a biker's nylon-lycra girdle,
the horn's on the other

bike, stored for winter, but
I'm honking, another PWA

on a borrowed bike, in a snowstorm

When Jim Died

When Jim died Joe did not want
Mention of AIDS in the news.
Marvin wanted a closed box.
Patrick, a military funeral.

We bury our living before we
bury our dead.

When Larry died we all wore
Three piece suits and sang
Church hymns at Harvard-Epworth.
Larry's lover, passing as

Larry's best friend, got up and
Spoke on Larry's culinary skills
And Larry's closest woman friend

Told how Larry had died with her
And her hubby in the suburbs, while
Larry's boss spoke of his skills,

Expertise with textiles. Gerry Sawyer
Asked the minister if Larry attended
This church, the minister said, He

Came to our old movie series Gerry
And I said That's nice and admired the
Woodwork and then Gerry was dead and

Jim was putting flowers on the bronze
Memorial erected by the City
To remind people Gerry'd lived there.

They misspelled his
Christian name.

March 1987

Talking to Jim

So nothing is left of your agony.
Already your friends remember
your service, splendid occasion.
Your final lover talks only of

you, everyone's pleased he has
a new friend. <u>Your sister's</u>
<u>defying your will, trying to</u>
<u>have you declared insane, adding</u>

<u>you were trying to go straight</u>.
I remember when KS reached the
tip of your nose *I'll never be*
ready for my close-up now, you

said in the living room. No one
was reaching for the camera.

3 September 87

The Robert Mapplethorpe Quartet

1.

We traveled in different circles
with limited overlap. I never

met Patti Smith, but we both
obsessed over men & flowers

Yours was the clinical eye,
the eye that saw the shadow

of the orchid, one of the "non-
innocent flowers" or, as you

called them, "New York flowers."
Your portfolio is filled with

New York flowers, and people
doing things some people did

 in the 1970s, wearing things
some of us wore when life

was limitlessly celebratory
and seemingly endless

2.

The Only Obscene Mapplethorpe

is not the one of the little girl
who did not wear her panties that

day on the stoop nor is it the ones
of Jim pissing in Tom's mouth or

vice versa in Sausalito nor is it
the 1978 self-portrait of Robert

with the whip handle up his ass
nor the men engaged in fist-fucking.

The only obscene Mapplethorpe is
the 1981 portrait of Roy Cohn

Destroy it!—the way God took
the horrible original

3.

Robert Mapplethorpe,
as my AZT beeper went
off during my second visit
to your Perfect Moment
and while I was trying to find
the water cooler your innocence

came to me Your image was in
a small lounge on a tv screen,
students were studying you,
you were explaining your craft
with your animation limited by
your illness Your innocence

came to me (that what it is
when a poet sees a flower and
decides—no—*accepts the
decision*—that this is the
time to find a notebook and pen
to commit to memory—or to lose
—the poem—but meanwhile
staring wide-eyed and for the
first time at the inspiration)

—the innocence—you brought
to the subjects brought to you

The only criminal offense anyone
can ever charge you with dead or
alive your work collectively or
one at a time is that your death
prematurely closed an eye that
knew the exact moment at which
it was proper, it was natural,
to blink

4.

Patti Smith was on Amtrak
Track Four Location B
next to a billboard that
said Unexpected Flavor
and another one that said
On Track for Taste both
ads for Merits and she
looked across the tracks
at me & said: Have you seen
Robert? *Yeah*, I said, as
my train pulled out, closer
yet to Manhattan, *every time
I close my eyes*

September 1990

Twilight

Twilight blue has
ever been my
favorite time of day:

the gentle dwindle of
light, soft tones,
eerie even, evening's

well-appointed threshold
without the scary
contrasts of dawn & night

Brothers

Squirrel! Squirrel,
do be careful
We live in the world
shaking our proud tails
but share the roads
with car operators who'd
run us over You for being
a rodent, maybe with rabies,
me for being a faggot,
maybe with AIDS
Look both ways, then
climb a tree instead
Maybe there'll be a nut
Maybe you can
have some breakfast
or maybe you'll be
hungry—but alive
to seek another meal

Celebrating the State of Non-virus

In late February, one of the least favorite stages of my least
favorite season I came down with a virus, not *the* virus which
I've already known since 1986, but a virus people get and talk
about on tv and at work and on buses. Having *the* virus I never
take a virus lightly, as the virus intensifies the minor discomforts of
life, and one never knows. One night I am at the theatre, laughing at
Harvard boys in drag, then my sleep is broken by the reality of shit in
my Calvin Klein button-down sleeping drawers, I get up and wash
them out and have 40 bowel movements, if one can call the whoosh
whoosh of hot brown water bowel movements, and why not, it comes
from the bowels! and it *moves*.

Well there is a virus going around, says my blasé doctor, and some-
times it is gone in 24 hours and sometimes, like with Dennis from my
group, who also had *the* virus, one can shit one's self to death, and
one does not know which this is until one morning one awakens after
actually sleeping without Halcyon and/or shitting ones favorite
undies. *Take nothing for granted.*

I do not want to die, and I certainly do not want to die shitting.
I've spent several years peeking into death preparation! and I know
Dennis's death was not a good death. A good death? Thurston said
in group one day, and one could almost feel the snicker in the
room, oh he is not only HIV negative, he hasn't read Stephen
Levine, he hasn't listened to Ram Dass, he probably hasn't even
had to try to embrace *this is not my pain this is the pain.*

Well, maybe I could forget this distinction too, if I didn't wake
up every day happy and surprised that, with or without pain, I am
still here, and Michael is beside me, and the cat wants her

breakfast. *Take nothing for granted.*
If piss flows through the penis, without pain, your pain or the
pain, show gratitude. Do not think, I used to bend over this
chair for pleasure, now I do it to put salve in my tired hole,
so sore, so sore. Tonight in the tub I fantasized dreaming, and
I was woken by a phone call from my mother, saying, "Walt, they've
found the cure." She was so happy, so grateful for the thought
that she might not survive me. "That's nice, Ma," I said, and sank
down into the mixture of Aveeno, Epsom Salt and baking soda.

February 1992

Garden Mystery

The snapdragons are missing
The snapdragons have

disappeared. Where are the
mostly white blossoms with the
cranberry innards? Choked out

by the Impatiens? The red the
white the variegated Impatiens
virtually indestructible until

the first frost. But now it is
midsummer: The snapdragons are

what is missing. It is I
who miss them

Chance

An umbrella fell. There
were several, hanging

from a doorknob. "Time is
the issue," said Dr.

Cooley, "we don't know how
long it will take for your

amylase level to go down.
I don't think you should

be off an anti-retroviral
for more than eight weeks."

When I got home I showered,
used Australian Miracle

Shampoo and conditioner,
as I left the bathroom in

my hooded crimson terrycloth
robe the umbrella fell. It

was my umbrella.

I dreamed

I dreamed everyone
came back. Some

chose to return
healthy, one had to

exercise memory
to remind of name;

some came back with
marks of illness, stamped

by disease's design.
Everyone was applauded,

appreciated, re-
acclimated. It was,

after all, a miracle.
It was, after all,

a dream.

virus cutting

virus cutting me short—
yet here I am with
some show tune in my head. So insistent

so splendid a lyric I can't
              get back to sleep

This is a battle cry. I

put a Bach tape on the
bedside boombox, try to

calm this hero, this warrior
queen, this Long Island
movie usher My armor's

a chartreuse teeshirt, my
agenda: to live

They tell us repeatedly that the
deadly virus is invariably fatal
Yet every morning drugged and
insomniac, queers filled with
toxicity and enchantment, fire
and fungus hear their voices,
then broadcast our own news

The Gentleman and the Lady in Me

for Ernie Schnell

When I decided to wear
the black polyester
peignoir to my 43rd
birthday party I
asked Ernie to come
to my room as I
switched from the
Dashiki I'd worn
for the lasagna part
of the festivities
to the babydoll I'd
purchased at the
thrift shop in
case this was
my final birthday
& I'd never get
to wear a garment
I've always wanted
to wear. Ernie
helped me find which
side was actually
the front, and after
we'd clasped the
gardenia corsage
to my wrist Ernie

opened the door for
me. I would have done
the same for him, & I
think we both knew,
that in a major way I
had opened the door
for myself

Coda:
Walta Borawski's Final Poem

Writing with AIDS

by Michael Bronski

In the fall of 1993—Walta was to die February 9th, 1994—I had to run errands, and, as was usual, a friend, Chris Wittke, stayed with him to keep him company and make sure he was safe. Walta's mental acuity was undimmed and his imagination flourished. Physically, he was very unsteady—always in danger of falling—and his motor skills such as writing had diminished considerably. He and Chris were on our second floor back porch as a storm was approaching. Walta asked for a pen and paper to write a poem. As he started writing it was clear that his fingers were unable to hold the pen to form, on the page, the words in his head. Chris offered to transcribe the poem on a separate page as Walta struggled to write it with his own hand. What follows here is Walta's poem as he wrote it along with its transcription.

It is not a very good poem. It has none of his elegance, his deep feeling for language, his humor, his irony, his anger, and his intelligence in it. But it is—purely and simply—a poem written from the vantage point of living *with* AIDS. It literally manifests his passion for writing. His desire to communicate, his need to express himself—no matter what—is quite simply visible in every line, word, scratch, mark, and scrawl.

[Michael I miss you so much]

as dictated to Chris Wittke

Michael I miss you so much
the storm makes me miss you
more than ever
Please
Please come home to me
And keep me warm
In this scary winter night

The night is too long
without you
Even the wind
(which normally I find comforting)
is just scary
without your arms

I miss you so much
Nights seem so
incredibly long and empty without you
("incredibly long and empty" boy is that
a bad line, but I mean it)
But at the moment even Harry's
exquisite food has not tempted you
home to my arms

When the
hours

M. you are
the first
I

I know that is hard
Person I
what you I miss it
with Great A
wisted it
Still
Still telling love.
Something else it.
more.

my life is short, but my hope for you is long...

michael — home —
come

un h they ther back,

michael, by des prhenne,
where please
are
you
Tim!?

Michael, please

I Ho how I
could
leave sir,

Michael —
standing for you

Michael —
I am
you are
then
over.

for my hundred happy...

Michael
make as
over & run,

Food is dull everywhere

scared machine.
hours — take

Afterword

Notes Toward a Memoir
by Michael Bronski

How We Met

The date was June 21, 1975. Walta was twenty-eight and I was twenty-six. Though we both lived in Boston at the time, we met—accidentally—at the Club Baths on First Avenue and First Street in Manhattan. Even more curious, we had both been at a mutual friend's birthday party two nights earlier, but had not been introduced, although I had noticed him and found him very attractive. I did not recognize him at the baths because I did not wear my glasses in the steam room. (How could I? They would have gotten all fogged up.) So, after hours of sex, I was indeed surprised and pleased to discover who I was with. As it turned out, Walta had also noticed me at the party and, seeing me at the baths, had followed me into the steam room. It was, as a friend noted years later when we told the story, almost fate. Walta and I were lovers from that day until his death on February 9, 1994.

When Did Walta Write?

During the time we were together, Walta wrote every day. He had always written; I have a manuscript of poems from when he attended Patchogue High School on Long Island in the early 1960s. After college, he became a staff writer and the arts editor for the *Poughkeepsie Journal.* When he broke up with the lover he had been with since they'd met in school, Walta moved to Boston to live with friends. He was unemployed when we met in 1975, and writing all the time, almost always poems. Wanting to do something less stressful than newspaper work, he took a job as a secretary at Little, Brown, then as personal assistant to the poet Denise Levertov (definitely not a low-stress situation). By 1979, Walta was the assistant to Dr. Ernst Mayr, the noted evolutionary biologist and professor *emeritus* at Harvard University. Dr. Mayr was European and valued having a male assistant, which fed into Walta's weakness for Anglo-European culture. He worked for Dr. Mayr until he went on disability, in 1992. (Dr. Mayr died in 2005 at age 100, publishing his final book months before his death.)

At each of his jobs, Walta found time to write. He wrote at home, and carried a notebook with him wherever he went. Writing, it seemed, was reflexive, as natural for Walta as breathing, eating, and talking. Easier, perhaps, than the last, for although Walta was a highly entertaining, engaged talker, that endeavor usually included other people and social interactions were stressful for him. As Virginia Woolf noted in one of her journals, every human interaction was a potential collision, a possible disaster.

What Did Walta Write With?

Fountain pens, mostly. He adored them, although he was also partial to medium-fine, rolling-point markers. He used violet ink—"Just like Ronald Firbank," he would tell people, then quickly add that he couldn't really read Firbank, because it seemed to be nonsense—and sepia, and sometimes (when he was in the right mood) a deep black that he thought looked impressive and bold. Once he mislaid an elegant fountain pen a close friend had given him, and the sense of loss was as heartbreaking for him as any medical diagnosis. We found it an hour later, but for that hour the pen—a beautiful, sleek green Waterman—was his health, his voice, his soul. He always had several concurrent journals, to fit into pockets or keep on his desk or just because he liked their covers. In a small notebook he kept the year before his death, he wrote: "Two new pens yesterday and new (violet) ink for my at-home pen today. I will use them all. I love writing."

Did Walta Write When He Became Ill?

As with any compulsive, Walta wrote more under pressure. The pressure to live, the pressure to become more known, the pressure to say something, the pressure not to collapse under the weight of fear and anger and pain. The pressure to make sense of the world, a life, an illness. The pressure not to give in, the pressure not to give up, the pressure not to surrender to all the pressure. Walta wrote in hospital waiting rooms, in sickbeds, in the car on the way to have a shunt placed in his brain to drain excess fluid that had collected, on our back porch when he could barely hold the pen because the pressure had built up and grossly affected his motor skills, sitting on a curb on the way home from Harvard Square because he had to stop walking because the nine blocks was too much to manage at one time.

What Did Walta Read?

Everything from Larry McMurtry's *Lonesome Dove* to Henry James to *Dr. Who* paperbacks to Jane Austen to Elizabeth George mysteries. His excitement over finding a new writer was equaled only by his passion for rereading and savoring again the familiar (he went into a reading frenzy when he discovered Caroline Gordon's Kentucky novels; his copies of Virginia Woolf's letters are riddled with underlinings in different colored ink, indicating successive re-readings). When he became too sick to read by himself, friends, or sometimes volunteer "buddies" from a local AIDS organization, would read to him. One not-very-close acquaintance who spent an hour or so with Walta told me afterwards that she was concerned that he kept asking her to repeat paragraphs; she thought his mind was going. I explained that he was just enjoying the book—which, by the way, was the third volume of Sigrid Undset's *Kristin Lavransdatter*. Walta vowed that he would finish the trilogy before he died, and he thought he did. (I had to shave off pages from every chapter when I read it to him, it is such a long book and he had such a short time left to live.)

What Music Did Walta Listen To?

The eclecticism of Walta's musical tastes was equaled only by his passionate responses. He was one of the few people I knew who could weep at Maria Callas singing Donizetti's *Poliuto* with the same fervor he brought to Emma Kirkby singing Handel or Ethel Waters singing "Suppertime" (whose version, even he had to admit, was as good as, if not better than, Barbra Streisand's). Walta was a diva queen and valued the emotional female voice above all. In addition to Callas, Streisand, Waters, and Mercer—all always referred to by their first names—Judy Garland, Nina Simone, Edith Piaf, Billie Holiday, Sarah Vaughan, Ella Fitzgerald, Alberta Hunter, Greta Keller, and Peggy Lee were in the pantheon. (But who doesn't love them?) Walta's indomitable curiosity pushed him to explore anyone who looked interesting.

This was when LPs could be bought for $6.95, so different from your average cost of CDs—$16.95—when they became the new technology; what could you lose? "Who was Mildred Bailey" he asked me one day when he brought home a three-volume set of her LPs. Luckily, she was great; I still play them today. But Marlene VerPlanck? Weslia Whitfield? Estelle Reiner (mother of Carl)? All great, and discovered only by Walta's neverending quest for new experiences. We were listening to the late Susannah McCorkle when her first LP was issued, because Walta liked the cover. (He would have loved YouTube and its amazing ability to resurrect even the most forgotten, neglected, and abandoned singers of the past century.)

But Walta's relationship to these women went deeper than mere sense of discovery or fervent reaction to their songs. Reading his poetry you can hear their voices—their timbre, their phrasing, their emotional nuance. Their anger, elegance, humor, and pain allowed Walta to experience and understand his own pain and loneliness before being gay became publishable, before the unspeakable became printable. While Walta read poetry—from Edna St. Vincent Millay to Robert Lowell, from Sylvia Plath to Adrienne Rich, from W.H. Auden and A.E. Housman to Muriel Rukeyser and Thom Gunn—the flame of his inspiration and poetic voice come, I believe, from American popular song, particularly as sung by women. "This is what our mothers grew up on," he would explain to guests at dinner who dared to wonder aloud why we couldn't play something, well, *newer*. And, once they'd accepted that, he would add, "Which is why we're so fucked up." (A fitting irony, I always thought: his own mother's romantic destruction by popular song as his salvation—an epigram waiting to happen, if it weren't so sad.)

Was Walta High-Strung?

Probably no more than most poets. Walta's desire to interact with the world—people, books, music, ideas, politics, sex, happiness, heartache—usually exceeded his immediate capacity to process the excitement those interactions generated. His pleasure at reading certain books, or listening to certain singers, would overwhelm him. He related heavily to the empathetic Mrs. Wititterly in Dickens's *Nicholas Nickleby*, who exclaimed, "I am always ill after the theater, my Lord. And after the opera I scarcely exist." (This quote—which is more of a paraphrase—remained on the bulletin board in our kitchen until I moved and is now in a box with many of Walta's papers, which will eventually be archived.)

Walta would weep while reading *The Portrait of a Lady*, and had an almost identical response to the ending of the *Star Trek* movie in which the trusty crew saves the whales by beaming them up to the *Enterprise*. Walta's intensity, and his intense appreciation of the world around him, fueled his writing; it was the root of it, the method by which he explained it to himself and the rest of the world—and the way that he defused his emotional evanescence.

Walta was as intense in getting his words onto paper as he was when he was explaining to you, eloquently and determinedly, why Mabel Mercer's version of "Clouds" was better than Joni Mitchell's (a dubious, if arguable, proposition), or when he angrily expounded on why *Kramer vs. Kramer* was insulting to women. The immediacy of Walta's emotions— what did happen to his superego?—is what makes his poetry still live and sing.

[Ed. note: An earlier version of this essay was published in The James White Review, *vol. 18, no. 3 (Summer 2001), edited by Patrick Merla.]*

Bibliographical Note

Sexually Dangerous Poet was published in 1984 by Good Gay Poets.

In their composition, the uncollected poems appear to pre-date the publication of *Sexually Dangerous Poet*. They are arranged chronologically by date of publication. The last four were published posthumously in 2003; their initial date of composition is unknown.

Lingering in a Silk Shirt was published in 1994 by Fag Rag Books.

Poems by Walta Borawski previously appeared in the following publications, occasionally in different forms:

Periodicals

Amethyst
Aspect
Bachy
Boston PWA News
Cat's Eye
Christopher Street
Dark Horse
Fag Rag
Gargoyle
Gay Community News
Hubris
The James White Review
Mouth of the Dragon
Northeast Alive

Outweek
PWA Coalition Newsline
Radical America
RFD
The Runner
The William & Mary Review

Anthologies

A True Likeness: Lesbian and Gay Writing Today (Sea Horse Press, 1980),
    ed. by Felice Picano
Anthology of Magazine Verse and Yearbook of American Poetry (Monitor,
    1981), ed. by Alan F. Pater
The Aspect Anthology: A Ten Year Retrospective (Zephyr Press, 1981), ed.
    by Ed Hogan
The Son of the Male Muse: New Gay Poetry (Crossing Press, 1983), ed.
    by Ian Young
Gay and Lesbian Poetry in Our Time (St. Martin's, 1988), ed. by Carl
    Morse and Joan Larkin
Poets for Life: Seventy-Six Poets Respond to AIDS (Crown, 1989), ed. by
    Michael Klein
Badboy Book of Erotic Poetry (Masquerade, 1995), ed. by David Laurents
The Name of Love: Classic Gay Love Poems (St. Martin's, 1995), ed. by
    Michael Lassell
Eros in Boystown: Contemporary Gay Poems About Sex (Crown, 1996),
    ed. by Michael Lassell
Flashpoint: Gay Male Sexual Writing (Richard Kasak, 1996), ed. by
    Michael Bronski
Two Hearts Desire: Gay Couples on Their Love (St. Martin's, 1997), ed.
    by Michael Lassell and Lawrence Schimel

The Columbia Anthology of Gay Literature: Readings from Western
    Antiquity to the Present Day (Columbia UP, 1998), ed. by
    Byrne R.S. Fone
Persistent Voices: Poetry by Writers Lost to AIDS (Alyson, 2009), ed. by
    Philip Clark and David Groff

The Library of Homosexual Congress, an imprint of Rebel Satori Press, preserves and promotes classic and provocative works of gay literature and nonfiction, with focuses on the AIDS crisis, the nascent gay rights movement as well as irreverent works of sexual culture and groundbreaking titles that deserve renewed attention.

Curated by Tom Cardamone and Sven Davisson

57082813R00168